Fragments of Stained Glass

Fragments of Stained Glass

Claire Nicholas White

Mercury House, Incorporated
San Francisco

Published in the United States by
Mercury House
San Francisco, California

Distributed to the trade by
Consortium Book Sales & Distribution, Inc.
St. Paul, Minnesota

Manufactured in the United States of America

Library of Congress Cataloging-in-Publication Data

White, Claire Nicolas, 1925-
  Fragments of Stained Glass: a memoir / by Claire Nicolas
White.
    p. cm.
  ISBN 0–916515–52–4 : $18.95
  1. White, Claire Nicolas, 1925 – Family. 2. White family. 3.
Netherlands – Biography. 4. United States – Biography 5.
Intellectuals – Netherlands – Biography. I. Title.
CT1158.W47A3   1989
973.9'092'2 – dc19   [B] 88-7843
                                                      CIP

To Sylvia

I would like to thank those who have encouraged and helped me to write this book, in particular Gunther Stuhlmann, Alden Cohen, Corona Machemer, Peter Shepherd, and Ellen De Maria.

Claire Nicolas White

PREFACE

If this book is a memoir, it is not necessarily history. The memory of a child is altogether unreliable, and it is not the veracity of what I remember as much as the why and the how that interests me.

My parents, Joep and Suzanne Nicolas, were artists. They belonged, when I was a child, to a period of intellectual bohemia in The Netherlands between World Wars I and II. Their two great friends, the poet Adriaan Roland Holst and the artist Dr. Henk Wiegersma, were towering personalities who have fascinated me all my life. In recent years, visiting Wiegersma's art collection in the museum in Deurne, I have come to realize what a tragedy their quarrel must have been for my father. Henk Wiegersma's own paintings struck me as more original and stronger than those of many of his contemporaries.

I suppose my parents' disorderly amorous lives have made of me something of a puritan. I found a refuge of privacy in the White family, into which I married. Their reticence was also a reaction to the dominant personality of my husband's grandfather, Stanford White. His murder caused my in-laws to shun the exuberant public life that seemed to have caused it. I have changed the names of some of the lesser-known characters in this book. In the interest of a more concise and formal structure, I have occasionally fictionalized details, but the chapter about our stay with the Huxleys in California is as accurate as I can remember it. Some names belong to history; others should be allowed to disappear into the shadowy texture of the past.

I
THE SACRIFICE

I first came to St. James, New York, my future home, in the winter of 1946. It was not a brilliant day of frost or a snowy day of soft white contours and silent roads, just a gray, cold day with nothing to recommend it. I arrived on a Sunday morning on the Long Island Railroad. The train's windows were dirty, the floors were wet, the heat rose in stale puffs from somewhere below my seat, and we were half an hour late.

I was a refugee, as most Americans are, or have been, or continue to be throughout life, moving from east to west, from north to south, from city to suburbs, always in search of a better way of life, a better place to be.

A twenty-year-old girl about to graduate from Smith College, I felt unsuited to the nomadic life and longed to be immersed in the thick soup of history. The war was like a bridge that I had crossed and that had blown up behind me. For the last six years I had, in my dreams, tried to cross that bridge again, to go back to my native Holland. But the

1

dreams would turn into nightmares. In them, I walked through my grandmother's house room by room and would come upon her bustling about, unaware of my presence. "Bomma," I would say. "Here I am. I have come back." But she ignored me, intent upon her occupations, locking and unlocking closets with the keys that dangled in a bunch from her belt as I had watched her do as a child. It was as if not she had died, but I, as though her world went on forever, no longer including me.

Sometimes I dreamed that I was taking the bus north from Alkmaar, the driver slamming the door open and shut as he called out the names of the villages: Bergen, Schoorl, Camperduin, always skipping Groet, the hamlet in which I was born. Anxiously I would look for landmarks—the brick roads, the post office, the café called *De Rustende Jager*—but all I saw were factories and smokestacks rising where meadows used to be. I'd wake up in a sweat and, starting all over again, try to do it right this time, to find the house with the thatched roof and the dark blue shutters, but I never did.

Now the war was over and the bridge had been rebuilt, but I had begun to realize that one cannot go back. The roots had been cut. I was a displaced person. At St. James station I took a taxi. I knew the name of my hosts, American friends of my parents whom I had never met. Ordinarily this would have made me wary, for I preferred my own expatriate friends in New York. But for some days now I'd had a premonition that this lunch would be important, that I must be sure not to miss it.

The taxi entered a white iron gate and drove up a long, mossy driveway between walls of rhododendron, their leaves drooping in the cold like limp hands. Those were the days when girls read *Rebecca* and *Gone with the Wind,* and inevitably visions of Manderley and Tara came to mind, houses that had been anchors and had then gone up in flames. This driveway led to a wide field, then to a house, a

fountain, Roman sarcophagi, and statues. The tall box-
wood trees were neatly tied together with string to protect
them from the weight of snow. Dogs barked and the front
door opened. One could see Long Island Sound at the foot
of the hill.

At once the atmosphere of this house, decorated with
baroque pillars, Renaissance mantelpieces and tapestries,
musical instruments, and Delft tiles, its walls covered with
leather-bound books, evoked memories of Europe. All
those transplanted objects looked at home here, assembled
with eclectic yet infallible taste. I had heard of the man who
had built the house. He had been a great artist, an architect
called Stanford White—a prominent and popular figure.
There had been a scandal about a woman and he'd been
shot by a jealous madman. This too evoked echoes out of
my past.

Now his numerous grandchildren received me warmly.
They appeared from all sides, dressed in warm sweaters
and drawing me to the open fireplace, for the large, somewhat dilapidated rooms were chilly. But the essential link
between my lost past and this place now appeared in the
splendid form of the artist's widow, the grandmother.

She came out of a door on the upstairs landing, the door
to what was called Grandma's Suite. She wore a wine-
colored woolen dress, its moth holes carefully mended.
Her white hair was up in a bun like my grandmother's, but
she was taller, more majestic, and her merry eyes had none
of the slight melancholy that hovered at the edges of my
bomma's expression. Seeing her, I felt at once that this
place could become home. Her ancestors had settled here
in the seventeenth century. The towns, the streets, were
named after them. "The land is mine as far as I can see,"
she used to say, deliberately blind to the already encroach-
ing neighbors. When I married her grandson she gave my
husband and me an old farmhouse on her property, where
I have lived for forty years. My four children were born

there and one is buried next to Grandma in the family plot. I shall join her there someday, for that is my logical destiny.

No doubt it was meant to be, this Americanization of mine, but it took my father to actually accomplish it. He shattered my past and I shall patch it together, as he assembled his art out of pieces of fractured colored glass. So long as I can keep going back, with the too easy pull of planes, with nothing more than an overnight bag, a ticket, a passport that betrays my origin, I will continue to cross the ocean, moving between present and past. I will keep my difficult balance between continents.

My children will never understand this. They take their birthright for granted and are at ease with it, whereas I have become a hyphen, a link. As I sit here facing an American field, I keep returning in my mind's eye to the garden in front of the house where my mother has just died, over there.

Between the moss-covered tree trunks stands a statue she made. It is of a little woman with a long skirt. She is leaning over, her hair touching the ground. Perhaps she is washing her hair in a stream. Her arms encircle the long tresses in a protective gesture. The entire figure, like the tree trunks and the wintry greens at their feet, is covered with a mossy organic sheen, as if this artifact had itself become a plant. With her hair, she seems to draw the sap out of the ground. Both her feet and her head have taken root.

Perhaps some day I shall be like her.

* * *

I was born in my mother's bed in our first home, which was paradise. My artist parents, running away from the stifling Catholicism of Limburg, had moved to the village called Groet in northern Holland when they married. The seventeenth-century farmhouse turned its back toward the sand dunes, but faced the polders, flat green meadows that stretched out to the horizon. A few miles north was the gap in the dunes where a dike had been built to keep out the North Sea, which, like an enormous wild beast, loomed above the land behind the fence of sod and stone, menacing yet fascinating. Nowhere else on earth was grass so green, as if it needed the nearness of danger to grow serene and fat. All day the wind swept the air clean, so that people breathed freely and never grew stale.

The beginning was utter happiness, as perhaps all beginnings are in memory. Then, in 1928 when I was three, something disturbing happened connected with the birth of my sister. The day before, my mother had painted the entire kitchen floor. I stood watching her from the brick-paved hallway as she crept, heavy-bellied, across the wooden floorboards that turned a glistening tile red under her brush. "Don't touch," she said. "Stay away!" Behind me Truus, our maid, stood over a steaming tub scrubbing sheets on a washboard. When she was done, she flooded the floor of the hall with whitish soapy water that ran down the brick gutter to the outside. "Watch out," she scolded. "You'll get your feet wet."

I was caught on an island and began to cry. "What a nuisance you are," grumbled Truus, lifting me with damp, wrinkled hands and releasing me outside on the grass, where a butterfly led me into the garden.

The next morning, I climbed out of my crib, which was painted Delft blue, and crawled onto Father's bed to wake him by prying open his eyes with cruel fingers. On the wall above his pillow hung a framed *Imagerie d'Epinal* of Christ mounting the winding road up Golgotha carrying His cross. A sad procession of friends followed along that ribbon road, and I traced the way with my index finger.

In the alcove stood Mother's bed, which was made of blond cherry wood and carved with swans' heads. It was like a sleigh drawn by the four birds, a sleigh in which Mother lay hidden. "I think it's coming," she called out. We both ran to her side, and with a reassuring wink in my direction she added, "Like a pip slipping out of a melon."

Hastily I was removed to the kitchen, and though the floorboards were shiny and dry by now, Truus would not let me crawl along them back into the bedroom. She ran about in a frenzy, her hair in disarray. Father picked me up in his arms and carried me to the dining room window. "Look," he said, pointing to a bird flying over the steep roof, "a stork. It is going to drop a sister for you in the chimney." Distantly I heard an infant wail. He imprisoned me in my barrel-shaped high chair and vanished, leaving me alone and bewildered. Then a strange woman entered the room. I could not imagine where she had come from. She looked at me with dark, brooding eyes, sat down next to me at the table set for breakfast, and demonstrated how to cut buttered toast in strips and dip them into the yolk of a soft-boiled egg. The resulting taste was consoling, and *gourmandise* became a substitute for jealousy.

"The strips of toast are called soldiers," she explained, arranging them geometrically on one plate. All that day she remained at my side, as if trying to take Mother's place, but she seemed distracted, staring out of the window and sighing, tucking the strands of her bobbed hair behind her ear. The next morning again she comforted me with soldiers, then drew open a curtain in front of a closet. In staggering arrays on the shelves, mocha cream cakes stood waiting for the christening. Every neighboring farmer had sent one, as was the custom, but even the sight of the rich, buttery icing in such abundance sickened me, and everything grew dark for a moment, as if I were sinking into the abyss of the woman's brown eyes.

"Jeanne," Father called this stranger cajolingly, "Jeannon. . . ." When I saw him kiss her behind the ear, burying his nose in the curl of her hair, I asked, "Who is she?" He explained, "Jeanne is your aunt, your mother's older sister, just as you are now Sylvia's."

At first this infant sister remained a dim and distant object in her cradle. Sylvia . . . the name whispered like that of my mother, Suzanne, whereas the sound of *Jeanne* was caressing, silken. Older, younger, perhaps sisters and aunts were echoes of each other. Then Jeanne left on the bus and we were once more a family unit.

Every night when the wind from the North Sea grew menacing and besieged the house, Truus would go out and lock the shutters it had been tugging and rattling. Before dinner I had my bath in a tub by the stove. Father, smoking his pipe, improvised stories for me, every night telling a new installment, about a forest world peopled with gnomes. As I listened, the blue silhouettes painted on the tiles behind the stove began to march along the walls; they were small hunchbacked men wearing bloomer pants, carrying fishing poles across drawbridges toward windmills that captured the wind in their flailing sails. "The wind so wild that heaven's child . . ." were the first words of a song Truus sang in the kitchen, and we could hear the wind prowling ominously over the dark dunes and polders, moaning in the chimney like a sad dog. Sometimes, upstairs under the thatch, it would pry open the door through which the hay used to be stored in the loft, banging and slamming it with all the violence of the night world we had shut out.

Then Truus served supper under the bare lightbulb shaded with a green glass that lit the table but left the rest of the room full of shadows. Mother joined us, round as a goddess, hastily buttoning her shirt after those long, silent sessions of nursing the baby in the darkened bedroom during which I thought Sylvia was eating her alive. At mealtimes, I too felt carnivorous and would gladly have eaten my parents so as to make them entirely mine. For a whole hour I could now contemplate my mother, who had been constantly eluding me behind closed doors. A Belgian, she spoke French rather than Dutch, and was finer boned than the other women of the village, sturdy

Frisians with water-blue eyes and hair as blond as flax. She was exotic, dressed in a vast sweep of culottes or, when walking through the streets, draped in a long gray cape. With the help of our neighbor she planted what she called an English garden, and she taught Truus to cook an Italian dish called *fritto misto*.

In the daytime, behind the studio door, the grown-ups led a life from which I was excluded. I stood watch at the garden gate for hours, sucking the red skin of the rose hips and staring at the polders, which swam off hazily toward the horizon in a blurred, damp curve around the world. Toward noon horse-drawn carts came by with vegetables and flowers or vats filled with herring. These last smelled of brine and sliced onion. The gray filets were sold raw, pickled or swimming in milk. The vendor rang his bell and wiped his knife on his white jacket, which was streaked with bloody fish entrails. The mailman approached with the gentle whirr of his bicycle, alighted with a flourish and unlatched the gate. The bus ripened from a distance, came to a loud, wheezing stop, and violently threw open its door. Then it rattled on toward the beach, empty in winter, loaded with pink, noisy bathers in summer.

A little after noon the village children returned from school with a clatter of wooden shoes. Seeing me, the girls in their aprons would descend upon the garden like sea gulls, pick me up, and coo and exclaim over me. When they held me close I got a whiff of the acrid smell of classrooms. They sat around me on the grass, their black-stockinged legs stretched out, and one of them exclaimed, pointing to a minuscule insect perched on her knee, "Look, a flea!"

Now and then a man entered the garden with a few freshly caught fish. He'd stand by the kitchen door to bargain with Truus, who examined his catch without enthusiasm. He caught mostly flounder, but one day there was considerable excitement, for he had brought some live eels swimming in a pail. Father was consulted and emerged from the studio in his velvet painting jacket. "Yes, yes," he exclaimed, "we'll have *anguille au vert* for supper," though Truus looked at the beasts with disgust. At dinnertime a huge pot of boiling water stood bubbling on the coal stove. From a safe distance I watched Truus dip her hand into the pail and, brandishing the squirming snakes, dunk them in the pot. But the eels jumped out of the scalding water and slithered to the floor. Truus and I jumped onto the kitchen table screaming hysterically while Mother and Father crawled about on all fours to capture them. This time they held a lid firmly over the cauldron in which the eels struggled in vain. For dinner the creatures were served up to us, lying still and vanquished on the platter.

A poet habitually came to dine with us on Sundays, when we had chocolate mousse for dessert. He arrived punctually on his green bicycle just as Truus was setting the mousse in little pots on the windowsill to become firm. Elegant, nonchalant, with a walking cane hanging from his arm, his neck and shoulders moved in one piece, and when he raised his eyebrows he lowered his eyelids, wiping his nose with the silk handkerchief tucked into his breast pocket. A lock of blond hair fell over his forehead and his straight upper lip remained stiff when he talked. His subtle smile was irresistible, and it took me many years to disentangle the word *lover* from the word *poet,* for I thought they must refer to one and the same profession. By contrast Father, with his unruly curls and striped turtleneck sweaters, his loud outbursts of hilarity as well as rage, seemed dangerously ebullient at times. *"C'est une soupe au lait,"* Mother would say calmly. "He boils over like milk soup."

After poking me with his cane, the poet, whom we called Jany, though his real name was Adriaan Roland Holst, disappeared into the studio, where a mysterious rite took place. The grown-ups were having *apéritifs.* The door to this room closed with a latch my index finger was too short to lift. With the help of one of Father's walking canes from the wooden beer barrel next to the door, I could lift the latch and peek through the square hole at the level of my eyes. On Sundays Mother's culottes were white linen French sailor's pants. Her shirt, too, was white linen and her long black hair was smoothed back in a Spanish chignon. The poet would kiss her cheek with his straight upper lip and they would sit together on the sofa while Father poured drinks and squirted soda water out of a blue bottle. Sometimes Jany brought a record and cranked the Victrola, and he and mother danced the tango to it. All this, seen in brief snapshots as the latch lifted and fell, was like a movie of the twenties, and I was both the spectator and the cameraman, standing outside in the hall, my eye glued to the square hole in the door.

Two years later came a Sunday filled with drama. I am still trying to unravel its meaning. That morning, a woman wearing a blue dress with polka dots arrived on the bus, fell into Father's arms, and began to weep.

"Poor Nel, what now?" he exclaimed. "Don't tell me he went to Paris?"

"Did he go off with Jeanne?" inquired Mother anxiously, and the woman nodded. "He has left me for your sister," she sobbed. My parents looked concerned, took her to the studio, and closed the door. I took my post at the latch but could not understand what she was saying between sobs. When they emerged for lunch, she seemed composed and Father put the tea cozy on his head to make her laugh. Later we bicycled to the beach through the dunes, for I had kept watch in the garden and signaled them when a patch of blue sky was on its way. Sea gulls dove through the wind as we walked along the strand. The two women were deep in a conversation that the waves drowned out. Riding on Father's shoulders, I urged him to gallop along the scalloped edge of the water and he complied energetically, but on the way back he set me down on my own feet and encircled the woman called Nel with his arm. She took my hand and smiled at me. Her eyes were a limpid blue, transparent as water, whereas Aunt Jeanne's eyes had been impenetrable.

"I have a little boy your age," said Nel. "I have five children." Five! I looked up with disapproval at this champion mother who leaned with such abandon on my father.

"Where are they?" I asked.

"Oh, I left them in Deurne." Her voice sounded melancholy but resigned. I now began to worry about these abandoned children. Was it their father who had taken off for Paris? In that case, might Father not take off with Nel, and Mother bicycle off with the poet, leaving me alone to take care of Sylvia?

The next morning the mailman appeared very early, while we were having breakfast, and with an air of importance handed over a telegram from the runaway husband of our guest, from Paris. She blushed as she read it.

"Henk says to go home to the children."

"Nonsense!" said Father. "Let him come and get you." And she stayed on day after day, looking more and more worried. They all looked worried and jumped up whenever someone knocked at the door or when the primitive telephone rang.

On Saturday some extraordinary fish appeared, covered with iridescent polka dots. They were kept alive in a laundry bucket in the garden and swam round and round with a graceful slithering of the tail, pumping oxygen through their gills, their lips curved in a sneering smile. They were such delicate fish, I was told, that we would eat them for Sunday lunch with the chocolate mousse, in the company of Nel, Jany, and "someone who is coming from Paris."

The fish distracted me from my snapshots at the latch. I crouched by the bucket and watched them swimming in circles, miles and miles on the spot, breathing strenuously to keep alive until the hour of their sacrifice. They were mysterious and different from me with their scales, their cold blood, their undulating motion — objects of deep concern because they were destined for our table. They were alive, and by Sunday noon would no longer be so. I was ready to accept this as the necessary order of things, but nevertheless kept my watch by the bucket.

On Sunday morning the house hummed with expectation; a nervous electricity filled the air. Father kept walking back and forth from the studio to the kitchen, from the dining room to the bucket in the garden, checking on things, warming the wine, picking at fluffs of dust on the carpet. He twitched his fingers as he walked by without noticing me, and he made a big displacement of air, as if he wore a robe with a train. The bulk of him was reassuring. Surely such a strong man could be afraid of nothing.

"And the fish?" asked Truus.

"Have the court bouillon boiling. I'll give you a sign when to throw them in, about twenty minutes after the gentleman from Paris arrives."

Jany, the poet, came. The four of them retired to the studio, peering anxiously through the window every few minutes, I noticed, and I ran from the latch to the gate to the fish. Though so insignificant a member of this household, I nevertheless had a strong feeling of my responsibility and importance. I believed that if I did not keep a close watch on everything, the whole structure of life would collapse.

Cats were prowling closer and closer to the bucket, which was covered by a protective chicken wire. It grew later and later and I longed hungrily for the porous mousse, the blue opalescent plover eggs, the butter curls on the kitchen table, while Truus grumbled because the toast was growing cold and her free afternoon dwindling. Then a tremendous noise approached in a cloud of dust, and a huge man on a motorcycle stopped in front of the house. It was Henk Wiegersma, Nel's husband. He looked terrifying on his iron steed, dressed in a white cap and white suit, his eyes glistening in the sooty face when he removed his goggles. It was easy to tell that he was in a towering rage. He swept through the kitchen without a glance at the delicacies awaiting him, went straight to the studio, and slammed the door behind him. Truus and I held our breath in the kitchen, listening to the explosion of voices in the next room. Eventually her hands began to move about her work and I crept to the latch and lifted it ever so silently with a straight, round cane. There stood the stranger in the middle of the carpet, all in white except for the black boots into which his plus fours were tucked, hurling insults at my father. Their meaning escaped me. "You stole my wife," he cried. Father seemed outraged and began to shout back, "You abandoned her for Jeanne!" Their faces were red, as if they might explode any minute. Trembling with fear, I learned then and there to keep silent and out of the way when confronted with violence.

The poet looked sardonic, aloof. He stepped between the two now and then with a conciliatory gesture but was pushed aside impatiently. Then, his sense of humor getting the better of him, Father shrugged and, taking a wooden T-square from his drawing board, aimed it at the white giant as if it were a gun, pretending to shoot him with it. But this light-hearted approach threw the other into such a rage that he cried, "Pistols! I'll be back with pistols, if that's what you want!" and grabbing his wife by the arm he dragged her to the door, straight toward me. I hid behind some coats hanging in the hall as they swept by, then watched them from the kitchen door as they mounted the motorcycle, she in her fluttery dress and delicate shoes perched precariously behind him. Then off they drove.

When they had driven off, we sat down at the table on which Truus had put the plover eggs, the butter curls, the watercress, and the toast gone soggy, but no one felt like eating.

"Does he mean it?" asked my anxious mother. The poet assured her with exasperating calm, "I know Henk! He means murder."

Father, whose face had grown twitchy and red, exclaimed, "He'll shoot me. We must leave at once."

"How about Jeanne?" Mother looked from one to the other. "What will happen to her?"

"It's all her fault," cried Father.

"But why? Poor Jeanne, he swept her off her feet." I could see my aunt flying off in a great wind.

"It's those eyes," said Jany, and I remembered the drowning feeling, the sinking darkness.

"It's not fair," Mother protested. "You would have done the same, both of you." Hurriedly she left the table and Father stormed out after her. The fish had been quite forgotten and Jany winked at me in complicity as I greedily licked the last chocolate off my spoon, trying to drown out once more the desolation of abandonment.

Early the next day we fled. Our bundles had been packed, the shutters closed, the door locked. To a five-year-old all this made very little sense, but Wiegersma was known for the violence of his temper, and my father took his threat seriously. Still, I was sure that if only the delicate fish had been served up and shared by the entire company, if the right ritual had been performed, this quarrel could have been avoided. The nagging memory of the fish swimming round and round in the tub haunted me. In my dreams the North Sea broke through the dike, the wind tore open the shutters and howled through the rooms, and the cats pried open the chicken wire, devouring the sacrificial offering that might have prevented our expulsion from Eden.

2
MR. PIMPUT

Sometime before the appearance of the menacing man on the motorcycle, I had adopted a personal protector. This companion of my imagination became even more constant than my parents and was tailored exactly to my needs.

I had been asleep for an endless time in my blue bed in the house by the sea. My dream had taken the shape of the lullaby my tone-deaf mother sang as I fought off the coming night, a dreaded, deathlike parting from the world.

> Mother is up in the garden
> Shaking the apple tree.
> Father is down in the kitchen
> Baking a cake for thee.
> A sheep with white feet
> Is walking in the field,

Is drinking the milk so sweet.
Sleep, baby, sleep.

When I awoke, bewildered and still drunk with sleep, Mother was shaking my arm and Father's smile was ecstatic. I wondered what was expected of me. A dark creature was sitting on the railing that enclosed my bed. By the shaft of light falling in through the open door, I could make out its long, hairy arms and its glistening eyes. It wore a red skirt with a hole in it through which came a tail like an upside-down question mark. It seemed as sleepy as myself, rubbing its eyes and scratching its head with pink fingers. Indignant at my parents for interrupting the pattern of night to show me my first monkey, I turned away and closed my eyes. As I did so I noticed a man's hat and face in the doorway behind the bed. He may have been one of the many beggars who walked by our house on Fridays with hurdy-gurdies, bagpipes, and harmonicas. I could hardly make out his face in the dark, yet I knew that this was Mr. Pimput and that from then on he would watch over me, whereas I myself identified with the monkey in his charge.

In my parents' bedroom, under a glass bell, stood a bunch of wax flowers in a vase, and under them a strange little man in a yellow suit who lifted his hat if one pulled a string. I was not allowed to touch him, for the glass bell had to be carefully lifted before he was manipulated. My father would do this for me if I asked him, but his hands seemed big and clumsy beside those of the courtly creature saluting me so politely with his yellow hat.

"It's Mr. Pimput," I said.

"What?" asked Father, lowering his ruddy, sandpaper cheek to my level.

"Put on the lid," I said. "He might run away."

Not long after that we left the house in the sudden panic caused by the threats of Nel's husband Henk Wiegersma.

We traveled on a train. Mother wore her gray cape and
Father's pockets were full of money and tickets. My sister,
Sylvia, wiggled a lot and cried, to my embarrassment, but
Father paid great attention to me, leaning over to listen to
my endless questions. I asked him what was written on the
sign near the window and he told me it said "Forbidden to
Spit" in five different languages. I thought this most
unlikely and suspected him of lying.

I then became absorbed in the endless pale green landscape and the continuous rows of evenly spaced trees in the
meadows parallel to the train. Behind the trees a gentleman with long thin legs dressed in a yellow suit was running
fast, keeping up with us. He sped along without effort,
quite light-hearted, so that I felt no concern about his
getting tired. I pointed him out to Father and explained
that it was Mr. Pimput, but he seemed uninterested and just
said, "Oh yes . . ."

Reassured and flattered that Mr. Pimput should follow
me on this long journey, I began to wave at him and, to test
his constancy, I looked away from the window for long
periods. But each time I returned my attention to him he
was still running alongside us behind the trees. He accompanied me all the way to our destination, delivered me
safely to the house of my mother's grandparents in
Belgium, then disappeared.

The house in St. Truiden was called The Rose. One
entered it through the store, which faced the market. Here
bolts of cloth were heaved onto a counter, then vigorously
unfolded and snipped through with great scissors attached
with a chain to the belt of each saleslady. These scissors
flashed dangerously at me as I walked into the vast
ancestral house filled with strangers. Servants, aged great-
aunts and uncles, my grandmother, Bonne Maman, and
my great-grandmother, Emérence, from whom I had
inherited one of my five Christian names, all seemed preoccupied with something important. Upstairs doors

opened and closed, while I was left alone in a room with a glass roof.

In the back of the room a door opened onto a garden. A slate path led to two wooden doors with latches, framed by a wealth of pink climbing roses with bees humming among them. The wilting petals came off in clumps in my hand, silky and crumpled and browning at the edges. One of the doors stood ajar, and seeing a pair of men's shoes that I thought might be Mr. Pimput's, I pushed it open. A man was sitting there on a latrine, his pants draped about his knees, reading a newspaper that hid his face. I closed the door abruptly. This could not possibly be my friend and protector, for the position was undignified. But where could he have gone? The yellow leaves of the trees were falling, decaying and wet underfoot. I felt alone and lost, forgotten.

Behind one of the trees something yellow stirred, reassuring. It was Mr. Pimput beckoning me, but then from the house I heard my sister scream and Mother's voice calling me. She came running into the garden, followed by Bonne Maman, who said, "Put them to bed. Children do not like confusion." Long necklaces of pinkish glass that tinkled as she walked were draped down her front, but I did not dare touch them for she seemed aloof. Unsmiling, she preceded us into the house and up the stairs. There Sylvia and I were put on chamber pots in a room full of linen closets and a linen press. "Push," said Bonne Maman, but, contrary, I refused to produce anything for her and I was put to bed with Sylvia while it was still light outside, which was humiliating. I began to search among the Chinese pagodas and bridges printed on the faded yellow curtain. A man in a pointed hat was fishing from a little boat under the bridge. "It's all right," I reassured Sylvia. "It's Mr. Pimput, you see?" But she was already asleep, her thumb firmly anchored in her mouth.

The next morning I woke early to the clamor of the carillon and loud activity on the square behind the curtain. Pigs squealing, carts rolling on the cobblestones, stalls being hammered into place, and the general bustle of Saturday market banished Mr. Pimput once more. Downstairs, the farmers who had come to town crowded the store. Having ventured among the forest of legs that smelled of damp wool, I panicked and hid under the counter at which Great-Grandmother Emérence herself presided, making small talk with the wives, scolding salesgirls, pouring tiny glasses of anisette when a sale had been made.

Back inside the house I wandered from room to room, looking for whatever might link me to the house by the sea, sniffing the scent of mocha coffee, floor wax, camphor, and patchouli.

Upstairs I found Father lying in a bed covered with a red wool blanket. With a red ribbon, he showed me how to tie a knot around his finger, and I felt held by it, attached to him. He too looked neglected here, no longer the center of attention. Then he said, "Go. You'll catch my germs." I wondered if they were fleas, like the ones I had caught from the schoolchildren in Groet, but he said no, he had a cold and would remain in bed. Then he undid the knot and I was once more adrift.

At the end of the hall, behind a closed door, I could hear people whispering. A maid came running out of it, wiping her eyes with a corner of her blue-and-white-striped apron. Seeing me, she took me by the hand and led me downstairs to the kitchen, where Sylvia sat in the middle of the wooden table. She was being fed spoonfuls of porridge by a fat, adoring cook. Every now and then the cook wiped Sylvia's face with a white dinner napkin, then kissed her voraciously. I too longed to sniff the damp softness, the creases in her baby neck. "Sylvieke," they clucked at her and she opened her mouth wide like a bird while I, resenting her willingness to perform for all these strangers, sullenly dipped my slice of *kramiek* in a bowl of hot chocolate.

At last I could slip away to the garden, and there, behind the trees, Mr. Pimput was waiting for me. Though he remained at a discreet distance, obviously as shy as myself, he greeted me with a nod. "How do you do, Mr. Pimput?" I said, for he was a well-bred gentleman who appreciated good manners. Hiding behind a currant bush, I spent the morning making piles and patterns with fallen leaves, yellow and brown star-shaped hands, looking up now and then to be sure my friend was still there. "Who are all those people?" I asked him, pointing toward the house.

"Umbrellas," he said. "Hooks and eyes. Galoshes."

"Everything is black in there," I said and shivered.

At noon the carillon once more began to ring, the sounds of bells falling on my head like rain, and again my mother came to fetch me. "What are you doing?" she asked. She looked distraught, tugging me along, looking up at the grim stone house, the blind windows.

An endless lunch followed, with stiff, white folded napkins one could wear as hats, only no one smiled when I did. The forks and knives rested on queer silver bridges, the napkin rings could be rolled across the table, the salt rubbed into the wine spots to make pink mud. Afterward everyone gathered in the room with the glass roof, where, with cool dignity, Bonne Maman poured small cups of mocha coffee. Great-Grandmother Emérence put her feet up on a chaise longue and fanned herself with her blue-veined hand. Aunt Rose, Mother's youngest sister, who wore pigtails, winked at me, then picked up the sugar pot and licked the contents, demonstrating how the sugar coated her tongue and made it white. "What an example you give the child!" exclaimed Bonne Maman.

The women began to talk in French. The name Jeanne recurred several times, uttered disapprovingly. Then the

name Maria was pronounced over and over with reverence.
I began to tug at my mother's skirt. "Mammie, mammie,
who is Maria?"

"She is my oldest sister," she replied, then continued to
talk to her mother.

"Mammie, mammie," I insisted. "When will I see Maria?"

"She lives in England, across the sea. Her husband is an
important man."

Suddenly the women got up and left in a hurry. What, I
wondered, is an important man? My two great-uncles were
asleep in their armchairs, their legs outstretched in front of
them, their faces covered with clean white handkerchiefs.
The two men lay there so still and anonymous behind these
masks that I wondered if perhaps one of them might be
Mr. Pimput, and I reached up to unmask him. An arm shot
out and caught me. The sleeping giant sat up and the
kerchief slipped, revealing a mustache, curling bushy eyebrows, and the much too sanguine face of Great-Uncle
Georges Baltus. We faced each other in the silent room.
Then the huge hand released me and I ran out into the
stairwell, where I bumped into the black skirt of a priest.
Now the uncles too emerged and the general rush to the
forbidden room upstairs was irresistible.

There I found everyone gathered around a high white
bed on which someone lay hidden in the pillows. They all
knelt as the abbé intoned the prayers. I wondered if the
man in the bed, whose face was hidden from me, could
possibly be Mr. Pimput, so I stood on tiptoe to catch a
glimpse of him, but of course it wasn't. An old man lay
there with a long sharp nose like a bird's beak and called
out in a loud, hoarse voice, "Emérence!" I thought it was
me he had called, that he was summoning me to join him in
the well of that white bed, so I screamed and screamed
until my mother carried me out of there. "What a nuisance
you are," she said, for I had caused her to miss the final exit
of her grandfather.

After the funeral, Aunt Rose undertook to entertain me with her marionette theater and the slides on her magic lantern. Landscapes in bright colors, children with enormous heads, gaudy birds of monstrous dimensions appeared on the wall, and finally there came a picture of a man running on skinny legs and holding scissors as big as those used to cut cloth in the store. "With those," Aunt Rose explained, "he cuts off the fingers of children who suck their thumbs. His name is John-the-Thumb-Cutter." But I knew perfectly well that he was Mr. Pimput and once more began to scream.

I ran out to the upstairs landing, which consisted of a balcony surrounding a central stairwell, an empty hole that plunged to the ground floor. There, feeling threatened by a dreadful danger, I fell and hit my head against the balustrade. Blood came spurting out of a gash in my forehead. My father came out of his room, picked me up, and carried me in his arms down to the kitchen, where he laid me flat on the wooden table like a chicken to be carved up and bathed my head with cold water. I heard my aunt laughing. "What a silly girl to be scared of a magic lantern," she said.

Furious, my face swollen with tears, I shouted between hiccups, "Mr. Pimput would *never* cut off Sylvia's thumb, you liar!"

For the next few weeks Father worked in Uncle Georges's studio at the back of the now wintry garden. One evening he came running in from the dark and cried, "I saw him, I saw his face in the window!"

"What?" Mother looked incredulous. "Nobody knows we're here."

"It must have been Mr. Pimput," I explained, but Father paid no attention and insisted we must leave at once, that he had been found out by his enemy, Henk Wiegersma, who had announced publicly to several friends that he was determined to shoot him. So this time we fled to Roermond, the home of his parents back in the south of Holland.

* * *

As Father pulled the brass doorbell of the ancestral house on a quiet, brick-paved side street, I could see meadows beyond, the late sun glistening on the river, and something yellow flitting by behind the rows of poplars. "How discreet," I thought. "He is keeping his distance, but he has accompanied me all the same." And so I felt safe in these new surroundings. While my parents unpacked and put Sylvia to bed, Bompa and Bomma Nicolas gave me a boiled egg to eat. This one was served in a blue Meissen egg cup and wore a yellow crocheted hat to keep it warm. They watched me adoringly as I cut my bread in strips. Their faces were *bons comme du pain*, as Mother said, good as bread.

We now settled in Bompa's house, though threatening letters from Father's enemy pursued him. Father had his photograph taken in a striped turtleneck sweater like that of a convict with a three-day beard and a sinister droop to his left eye, and sent it to Wiegersma half in jest, half as a threat. Wiegersma then changed his tactics. Slanderous articles began to appear in the papers. I could not read yet, but I heard the grown-ups talking about them. The newspapers also mentioned the famous kidnapping and murder of the Lindbergh child in America, and, playing alone in the garden, I was terrified of being kidnapped by Father's enemy.

This garden was surrounded on two sides by walls, then spilled out at one end onto the valley of the river Maas. It was here that Mr. Pimput and I became closely acquainted. Whenever I was afraid, he would appear in the distance, behind the trees, on the roof of the house, or running along the horizon. Only when I was quite alone would he come closer and start a conversation. Though an eccentric person, he never acted silly to attract my attention, as did some of my parents' friends. He never patted my head or winked in a condescending manner or rattled money in his pockets while rocking back on his heels, but treated me like an intelligent equal. His eyes were charming, sometimes lively, sometimes melancholy, and he spoke rapidly when trying to explain things to me. He taught me so many things nobody else knew that I wonder what I would have become without him. We discussed the meanings of words and wondered together about the Holy Trinity and about eternity, deciding at last that these were mysteries better left unsolved.

One day, as we walked along the river, Mr. Pimput disclosed his greatest secret. "Without you," he said, "the world is really not there at all. When you sleep there is no river, there are neither birds nor people. This is why you have to be very careful to keep good order in the world, observing everything so that it will continue to exist. If you forget to look at your father and mother they will not be, and so it is with everything."

I realized the extent of my responsibility and how difficult it would be to do justice to all creation, of which I was the absolute center.

"When I found you in my world," Mr. Pimput went on, "I thought it would be a pity for you to vanish, and so I came and watched over you so you would remain present."

* * *

When I was twelve, the time came for me to learn the things everyone knows and to live with other children at a boarding school. Until then, the local school had left me quite free to retreat to the company of Mr. Pimput, but now a uniform arrived for me, a straight black dress with a white collar and several pairs of long black stockings. I was wor-

ried and went to tell Mr. Pimput about all this. He said
nothing and looked evasively toward the horizon. I asked
him whether he was sad that I was leaving. He shook his
head, apparently resigned, and said, "I knew it, I knew it." I
pleaded with him, for I did not want to be left alone.

"You will come with me, dear Mr. Pimput, won't you? You
won't let me disappear from your world?" But he continued to shake his head and to murmur, "I knew it, I knew
it," and then, as I burst into tears, he left me, vanishing in
the distance of the landscape.

Two days later I was driven by my mother to a French
convent in Ubbergen. I never saw Mr. Pimput again, but
have, throughout my life, looked for substitutes.

When I came home that year for summer holidays, Aunt
Rose came to Roermond with her fiancé, a Belgian poet
named Eric de Hauleville. This strange little man had
pudgy cheeks, dimpled hands, and blue eyes with curly
lashes. His mouth could pout childishly at one moment,
then move miraculously fast the next to produce a cascade
of words, words that shone and were as smooth as pebbles,
as prickly as sea urchins. It mattered little whether I understood their meaning. He seemed to savor them on his
tongue and would try to communicate to me their flavor
until they acquired a definite taste of their own in that
other, still somewhat opaque French language. Quite deliberately, he seduced me with his art and his attention,
though God knows I was difficult to seduce. Suspicious and
solemn, I listened as he took me with him on his long
rambles through the countryside, treating me to glasses of
lukewarm beer at village cafés and to monologues on etymology and philology, as if I were his equal. Did he guess
the gratitude behind my persistent muteness, my unsmiling scowl? He wrote a poem about me, chose books for me
to read, and showed me where wild orchids grew in the
dunes behind Ostend. Painfully shy, I still resisted his
friendship, for it threatened to break down the safe barrier

behind which I hid. Eric was too real, too overwhelmingly
alive, and besides, I still thought then that houses, friends,
countries would belong to me forever, that life was bound
to be an addition rather than a subtraction, that there
would be plenty of time in the future to tell Eric that he had
won me over.

Much later, in the spring of 1941, when we lived in New
York during the war, a letter arrived from my Belgian
grandmother, Bonne Maman. With Rose and Eric and
their baby daughter and thousands of other refugees she
had fled the invasion of Belgium along the choked roads to
the south of France. During the hardships of this journey,
Eric's health, which had never been strong, had failed
altogether and he had died in St. Paul de Vence. "His illness
was painful and made life difficult for us all," wrote Bonne
Maman. "He was temperamental and restless and did not
want to die. He refused to see a confessor until the very last
moment, when he sighed, 'How easy it is.' And so his last
hours were calm. The almond trees were blooming in the
mountains. It was the day of Pentecost."

When I read this letter I said without thinking, "Mr.
Pimput has died." The real friend, this man who had
dazzled me with his inventiveness, who had tried with it to
enter the impenetrable world of childhood, had replaced
the imaginary one. Was it my fault, I wondered, that he had
vanished, since I had not continued to watch over him?

3
SHADOWS

My grandparents' house in Roermond was four centuries old and it was rumored that William the Silent had "slept there." It was one of the more elegant dwellings in a small provincial town, yet it was also uncomfortably cold and filled with awkward furniture and dark paintings of a period that is now frowned upon.

How can I explain the personality of that house? Probably ugly, gloomy even, it had so strong a mood that it seems ridiculous to apply standards of taste to it. It would not occur to me to say that I was happy or unhappy there, only that when I recall climbing the broad stone steps to the front door, peering through the mailbox, seeing the front hall paved with black and white stones and, beyond it, the door open on the garden, my heart beats faster and I feel, as then, on the verge of making a great discovery, of unveiling the secret of life.

The house, the entire neighborhood, was overshadowed by the cathedral. Like a broody hen it crouched protectively

over the streets clustered around it. My grandparents'
house, too, was filled with the mysteries of religion. When
the great church bells boomed, their vibrations filled the
very marrow of the rooms. Antique stained glass was set in
the windows of the parlor, the dining room, even the bathroom. Fragments of angels and saints, eyes, mouths, and
wings filtered the light of the street through brilliant colors.

Near the front door was a small parlor, where unexpected visitors were made to wait. On Fridays, when hurdy-
gurdies, street singers, and beggars were allowed to invade
the town, my grandmother would distribute her charities
in this room to a series of her personal mendicants. It was
here too that my sister and I were made to play if my
grandmother was out. On these occasions, a gas fire was lit
that glowed bright red in imitation of an open fireplace. A
spinning wheel with a red ribbon tied around the flax stood
in one corner and, dominating the room, looking down on
us with oppressive realism, were two paintings by my great-
grandfather: an Ecce Homo, the face of Christ dripping
with blood under His crown of thorns, and a Mater Dolorosa, the red-eyed virgin, her cheeks streaming with
tears.

The dressing table in my grandparents' room was an old
washstand with a pitcher of water set in a blue and white
china bowl. The slop bucket stood beside it. The wardrobes
were brown with squeaking doors. In the center of the
room, the vast bed loomed like a sacrificial altar, its four
posts nailed upon the four corners, rosaries draped over
the head. Under it stood a flowered chamber pot. At the
foot of the bed was the prie-dieu covered with purple velvet
on which my grandmother said her morning and evening
prayers to an ivory crucifix.

Most of our time was spent in the dining room, where my
grandparents sat for hours on end, each in a brown armchair, between them an enormous radio with a number of
buttons to be adjusted. My father had begun to breathe a

revolutionary life into the family stained-glass studio, enab-
ling Bompa gradually to retire. He would sit reading the
papers while Bomma knitted and Sylvia and I played with
boxes full of buttons or bags filled with remnants of wool.
Sometimes Bomma took a box of ivory dominoes from the
closet and spread them out on the heavy Persian rug that
covered the table. Then we gathered in the island of light
that fell from the overhanging lamp and tried to play the
game according to the rules. I was now in first grade, old
enough to know the patterns of dots by heart, delighting in
their black-on-white symmetry as they grew into a long
snake over the carpet. At times I managed to outwit
Bomma, but Sylvia inevitably disrupted our game. With
violent outbursts of rage when one of us won, she swept the
dominoes onto the floor, screaming "No fair, no fair!"
Then creeping under the table between its lion paws to
retrieve them, she tickled Bomma's ankles and pulled at the
tassels of the carpet, once more disturbing our patterns.
Frustrated, I kicked her till she set up a howl.

At dinnertime Anna, the maid, entered. She put coal on
the stove, removed the Persian rug, and covered the table
with an oilcloth, a felt pad, and then a white cloth. On
Fridays the buttermilk soup with molasses sickened me, but
on Sundays the tantalizing smell of broth hung over the
house. It was Bomma's specialty, and when her three sons
came by on their way back from church, this smell would
draw them to her for a prolonged visit. They were then
served a cup as an advertisement for the evening meal, and
seldom could they resist the invitation to Sunday supper.

The family gatherings were dreary yet soothing. My
grandparents' three irascible sons would gather around the
table with their families, and the jokes and quarrels were as
monotonous as the menu of broth with marrow balls,
homemade bread, smoked beef paté, and salad, followed
by fruit compotes or enormous rice-pudding tarts. Before
the evening ended my grandfather and his sons would be

hurling not only insults but napkin rings, forks, and spoons (nothing breakable; they were too stingy for that) at each other across the room as their voices rose and their blood became heated by the excellent wines. At the head of the table sat my little grandmother, dressed in black, resigned and bewildered under her snow-white hair. To her, this was all part of the vale of tears into which man is born to love.

Into this life full of shadows, Mother entered like a blaze of light. Impatient with conventions, imposing her will to be happy, she soon introduced subtle changes here and there that made the house a pleasanter place to be. Gas stoves were installed in the bedrooms, so that the water no longer froze in the washstands; the dust covers were removed from the parlor furniture and the wooden shutters opened to let in the day; the maid was given a blue uniform instead of her sweaty black dresses; and in the garden a rockery, a pond with goldfish, and a statue spouting water now enlivened the formal labyrinth of narrow gravel paths bordered with low box hedges.

Mother must have seemed wickedly worldly to the rather grim little town. She was slender and well dressed, spoke French, and wore lipstick. When I walked through the quiet streets with her, boys followed us, threw stones, and shouted insults at her, as if she were a sinful woman. This filled me with indignation, and I would have fought them off if I had been bigger and less shy.

It was with Bomma that I loved to go to daily Mass in the morning very early, when the stars still hung over the street. On Sundays, sitting at High Mass beside Mother, I would get too distracted to become absorbed in the poetry of the music, the candles, the incense, and the ancestral stained-glass windows. Anxiously I watched for the moment when, her head nodding ominously, she woke up with a start and, lifting her hand to wipe away the little drop forming at the tip of her nose because of the cold, sent the change held ready for the collection flying across the

church with an unseemly clatter. This embarrassing inci-
dent was repeated Sunday after Sunday until I managed to
convince her to let me hold her money.

Mother's studio was on the second floor of the house.
There she stood for hours on end in her pale blue smock at
her modeling stand, a ball of clay in one hand, touching up
the surface of the statue with the other. Then, moving back
a step, she leaned her head sideways to look at the result,
too absorbed to notice Sylvia and me if we came in to
plague her with our quarrels. At times her life-size saints
collapsed overnight, their armatures inadequate or the clay
too wet. Both she and Father went through a phase of
joyous bacchanalia, in which all their figures danced, held
birds, sang open-mouthed, waved their arms, or ate
grapes.

Father moved between his upstairs studio, where he drew
cartoons on a huge drawing board, and the glass studio in
the garden, where the windows were cut, painted, and fired.
The workmen, wearing long gray smocks, walked back and
forth to a storehouse across the street carrying sheets of
glass on their shoulders. They sometimes stopped and
joked with us, but Father always seemed preoccupied and
flicked his nervous fingers behind his back when taking a
quick turn around the garden. So my parents worked
behind closed doors for long, silent hours, and we tiptoed
from one to the other, always ending up at Bomma's, for she
was always there, always reliable, looking up from her knit-
ting to welcome us. It was she who watched over our colds
and whooping coughs. When I was critically ill with bron-
chial pneumonia, she sprinkled Lourdes water over my bed
and slipped a relic of St. Thérèse of Lisieux under my
pillow. Mother seemed annoyed at this. It implied that there
was actual cause for worry, that my life was in danger, which
she refused to believe. She brought me flowers, toys, and
exotic fruit, performed puppet shows at my bedside, and
when I was delirious she laughed and said, "You're talking

nonsense!" so that I pulled myself together and soon got better.

Mother was just beginning a subtle campaign to introduce some light gray, flowered dresses into Bomma's wardrobe to replace the solid black when suddenly, without warning, Bompa fell dead at the breakfast table. That day, all the shutters were once more shut tight, the dust covers returned to the parlor furniture, and my grandmother, in deepest mourning, was herself the image of the Mater Dolorosa. There was nothing mournful about Bompa, however. Laid out in a starched, pleated nightshirt in the little parlor with the spinning wheel, he looked peaceful and content.

After this setback, it took my mother a good two years more to convince Bomma that pale, flowing dresses and open shutters would not be judged as frivolous by the town. The garden had become her center of operations. A lazy lawn replaced the stiff paths, and flowers appeared everywhere, grouped casually in the English manner. In summer, tea was served daily under the plum and apple trees, and the fruit rained about us with abundance as we sat with Bomma, whose expression of resignation gradually changed to one of peaceful happiness.

One by one the rooms were painted in pale pastels, the carpets disappeared from the tables, the bunches of Judas penny from the bedrooms, the buttermilk soup from Friday's menu. The house lost most of its character, but it was up-to-date and in the best of taste. Parties with Chinese lanterns were given in the garden, cars drove up to the house from Brussels, Paris, and Amsterdam. Visitors paid their respects to the gentle old lady whose home was now filled with noise, children, dogs, piano music, and light.

Then, while I was away at boarding school, Bomma became very ill. It was apparent that she would not survive an operation, and I was allowed to come home and take my leave of her. My mother met me at the station and explained all this in the gentlest possible way, so that nothing would seem harsh or at all disagreeable about this death. It was as if she were fitting it all in with the interior decoration. But as soon as I entered the house, I was aware of untidy undercurrents, explosive conversations behind closed doors. A great-uncle with a red mustache, much given to histrionics, received us with exclamations of despair.

"It's that impossible maid of hers. She took the letter to the hospital. Imagine!"

"What letter?" my mother asked.

"The one from Charles!"

"How could you be so careless!" My mother was furious. She had always been annoyed by this bachelor from Brussels, who used to come for prolonged visits to drink up the best wine in the cellar and take a local schoolteacher dancing at a place called the Harmony Bar. "Don't you know what it said? I'll quote it to you word for word. 'Is it really true that there is no more hope? Is she really doomed to such a cruel, painful death?'"

"I know, I know! But how could I foresee that that maid would take it to her with yesterday's mail?"

"You should have burnt it, torn it up, anything. Has the girl come back yet?"

"No. She went on the bus."

Mother put her hat back on and grabbed me by the hand.

"It may not be too late yet," she said and off we drove at full speed to the hospital in our American car, one of the first automobiles in town.

In her little room, Bomma lay staring peacefully at some flowers, which I recognized as one of mother's helter-skelter bouquets. Her pink, round face was framed by the foam of white hair and she wore a pale blue bed jacket trimmed with lace, obviously something Mother had provided for the occasion. Above her head, however, hung a container from which a tube disappeared mysteriously inside the bed. "Intravenous feeding," Mother told me later, but now she started talking with a strained cheerfulness that embarrassed me. "Ah, how well you look today! And that jacket looks so fresh. Claire has come to see you. She had an unexpected vacation from school."

She pushed me from the back and I approached the bed with my usual dread of disease, but to my relief Bomma's cheek had the same flabby silken consistency I loved. She did not speak, but looked at me with tired eyes that glistened darkly behind the drooping lids and I longed to tell her, "Bomma, Bomma, I will live in your stead, I will take your place, I will be you." Mother in the meantime chattered away.

"The doctor says you can come home next week. Isn't that wonderful? We're having a double door put on your bedroom so the children won't disturb you. Anna's sister will come to help out and take care of you until you're up and about again. Oh, you should see the garden now! I had a bed of those red and yellow tulips you love planted under your window . . ." I could see Mother's hand moving stealthily toward the letters on the bedside table. Then casually she added, "Have you read your mail yet? Would you like me to read it aloud to you?"

Bomma looked at her with a resigned smile. In a voice that seemed fatigued and remote she said, "But why do you keep pretending that I am not going to die? Don't you know I want to be prepared to meet my Maker?"

Startled, Mother looked up. She seemed confused; she even blushed. Suddenly she looked like a little girl, quite lost, defeated. On Bomma's face there was now a slight smile of irony and triumph, which made her the winner in this match between light and darkness. Flustered, Mother got up and pulled me out of the room. As she walked ahead of me with large strides down the echoing hospital hall, I could see her wiping away the tears with her coat sleeve.

4
THE BARONESS

Roermond was Bomma's home. She had lived in it, secure in her position. But growing up there, I began to notice the complicated maneuvers by which people strove to climb the social ladder.

Around the corner from our street lived the baroness, a mysterious person whom nobody knew. Her house filled almost the entire block and its door was guarded by a butler in a pink-and-white-striped jacket. There were other, minor barons in our town. There was even a count, who lived in a nearby castle with a drawbridge and a moat, on which we were allowed to skate in winter. But none of these was shrouded in such exclusive mystery as the baroness. It was rumored that she was a lady-in-waiting to the queen, that she was away a lot. The navy blue shutters to the street were often closed. We whispered about the contents of the house as we walked past it on our way to and from school. Someone had seen the chandeliers lit at night. Another had seen the butler carrying a silver tray with crystal glasses, but no one, not even the Chinese doctor with nine children who took care of all the best families, had ever entered the baroness's house.

Then, one day, all the shutters were opened, suitcases were carried into the house, cars stopped, and the baker delivered vast amounts of the crisp rolls that looked like babies' bottoms and were called cadets. The housemaid, who had gone shopping at the butcher's, volunteered the information that the baroness's grandson, recovering from a lung condition, had come to spend the winter. To entertain him, the baroness had invited the royal children of Belgium. This news created great excitement among my friends on the street, which was rather disillusioning to me. I had thought of us as a totally democratic gang of free individuals, unconcerned with social conventions.

On the street, I was rough and loud. By second grade I knew which cobblestones were missing against which school wall, where one could excavate some dirt in the sidewalk to make a "pot," who had the newest marbles. Armed with a cloth bag full of brown clay marbles and with a gambler's instinct, I played the game of *knikkeren* till dusk. I took to the streets first on wooden stilts, then on a scooter, roller skates, and, at the age of nine, my first bicycle. On this last I explored the marketplace, the city walls, the chapel of the Carmelites, the railroad station, the bridges across both rivers, the forests on the German border. During the summer holidays I went swimming in the muddy swamps and gathered water lilies; in the wheat fields, I picked bunches of poppies, cornflowers, and camomile. After whole days of wandering with a sandwich in my saddlebag, I would come home exhausted and happy, my bag full of chestnuts. As I entered the house followed by the cool smell of evening air, the way a dog drags his wanderings behind him, Mother would ask with moderate interest, "Where have you been?" But I was vague and private. My friends out there and I had formed a secret

society, pricking our fingers to become blood sisters, or
rather brothers, for we were still at an age of genderless
adventure and thought of ourselves as wild American
Indians.

In spring I loved the sound of the heavy, white hemp
rope slapping the dusty ground and the chanting of our
jump-rope song:

> My father has a parrot
> That sings an odd song.
> It sings this, it sings that,
> Eighty years long,
> And Mieke turn around.
> Mieke here, Mieke there,
> Mieke in America.

My favorite cousin was called Mieke, which made the
song all the more intriguing. America obviously was a
country full of parrots, but how Mieke had gotten there
puzzled me. She was two years older than I and paid little
attention to me, but at the rumor of the royal children's
arrival she came and explored the wall that separated
Bomma's garden from that of the baroness. I followed her
example and scaled the wall behind her, peering at the
immaculate lawns and formal flowerbeds, empty now in
winter. After this, Mieke enlisted my participation in
various ruses, such as falling off our bicycles on the street in
front of the elegant house or pretending to twist our
ankles. Several times I caught a brief glance through the
curtains of the parlor window of a dowager figure with a
sloping bosom and three strings of pearls, but no one
emerged to rescue us.

I could not quite understand Mieke's fascination with the
baroness, but I was flattered by her renewed interest in me.
When I had started going to school, at the age of six, Mieke
had been delegated to walk me back and forth through the

streets, a job she had at first taken to heart. Soon, however, she had become embarrassed by my rowdy behavior, especially my impassioned game playing, during which I often accused my playmates of cheating. I shouted insults in local dialect and got involved in fights. I was always one of the last to head for home. My hands were usually numb with cold, my hair in a tangle, my stockings drooping in a wrinkled bunch above my shoes, and my woolen underpants, knitted by Anna, falling down below my skirts.

Three years later it became my duty to drag Sylvia along. I blushed at her runny nose, hoisted up her woolen pants, and tied her shoelaces on windy streetcorners. Full of admiration, I watched Mieke from a distance as she bicycled by among swarms of classmates, dove from the highest diving board, or skated figure eights on frozen flooded meadows. Someday, perhaps, I would be as free as she was to move in ever-widening circles. The phrase *Mieke in America* came to mean total independence.

And so I was pleased to be enrolled in Mieke's assaults upon the privacy of the baroness. Her next ploy was to organize a daring group of St. Martin's day carolers. Singing in close harmony and carrying paper lanterns, they rang the polished copper bell of the baroness's house, but when the door actually opened and the butler appeared, shyness overtook them. Their voices quavered and their song sounded shrill and thin. I stood waiting at the corner to hear what they had seen. They had been handed meringues and figs, they had actually entered the front hall, and a boy had come out of a room and stared at them. "He was skinny," Mieke said. "Perhaps your age. He was blowing bubbles with his spit."

"Was he a prince?" I asked. "Was he one of the royal children?"

"How should I know?" she shrugged. "They don't exactly wear crowns."

I would have forgotten the baroness if my Belgian grandmother had not been indirectly responsible for introducing me to her. Periodically Bonne Maman came from St. Truiden to see to our education. She stood over me as I did my homework and gave me lessons in calligraphy. The slanting, dainty script with curlicues on the capitals that the Dutch nuns taught she considered vulgar. I must learn to have a round hand, *à l'anglaise*. In fact, Holland was inferior in all ways to Belgium, where manners were more refined and French was spoken. No doubt the baroness spoke it too. Flemish, like Dutch, was the language of peasants. Culture required French.

Because of my republican predilection for the rabble, Bonne Maman decided I needed the full benefit of her attention. She saw to it that I got piano lessons and made sure a strong lamp lit the page from the left side when I drew, my pencils were sharpened and soft, and my paper was thumbtacked to a slanted drawing board. By the time she had installed me, all my initiative was gone and I had a stomachache. As I gasped for breath, her eagle eye noticed at once.

"Something is wrong with that child," she said, and decreed that there would be no more mayonnaise for me and no more chocolate mousse. She forbade just those delicacies that had been prepared especially for her visits.

Bonne Maman's perfectionism, her willpower, and her demands created a tension in the house. Anna grew cross, Father irascible, and my mother, her own daughter, looked small and obedient, always agreeing as the toneless, monotonous voice gave instructions on nutrition, hygiene, and table manners. *"N'est-ce pas . . . ,"* Bonne Maman repeated over and over. *"N'est-ce pas . . ."* Nespa, nespa, like a wasp, I thought, and it struck me that she was rather the baroness's shape, large-bosomed with low-cut fronts.

"She made us what we are," Mother argued in defense of

her. With this she implied that if we were at all remarkable it was Bonne Maman's doing.

Culture had been the consolation of Bonne Maman's life. Her brother Georges, the artist, had been her idol. Her daughters had all married "great men," artists and writers who had lifted them out of the merchant's world from which she came. "She is a woman who created daughters to make men work," complained her sons-in-law.

Her own husband did not work. She was the daughter of linen merchants, he the heir of a wool factory. There is an old adage in Flanders that one must never marry wool to linen. The result of this match was bankruptcy, after which my grandfather, a sweet, gregarious man, spent the rest of his life playing cards and drinking beer. He died early, having broken his neck in a fall as he came home from the café one evening. It had been a scandal. Bonne Maman had cried every morning at breakfast, Mother told me. She consoled herself by reading the *Revue des Deux Mondes,* to which her brother Georges subscribed, and with the string quartets he imported now and then from Brussels to give private concerts in his studio.

After the feast of St. Martin came that of St. Nicolas, when we traditionally received presents. That year, the year of the baroness, Bonne Maman brought me piles of gilt-edged, red-bound books illustrated with engravings of the ruins of Rome, typhoons, and the Seven Wonders of the World, books that had been her own as a child. I pored over these and marveled at what was awaiting me out there, beyond the streets of Roermond. Another present, however, caused me much distress. It was a horrible live rook she had found in a ruin along the road from St. Truiden. It had a broken wing and stared at me with nasty beady eyes, pecking at my fingers with its coarse beak when I fed it. Father named it Cornélie, and for some reason assumed that I adored it. I had to feed it and put water in its cage, but when it croaked at me and beat its wings I panicked and ran away, leaving the door to the cage open. The first time it escaped, it hopped to the little pond with the goldfish in the garden and fell in, setting up such a racket that the workmen came running out of Father's studio. They fished it out, wrapped it in a piece of red flannel, and gave it gin to drink. Cornélie revived and began to caw so drunkenly that everyone found her charming except me. I wished she had drowned.

No sooner had her wing mended than she escaped again, flew into a tree, and from there to the baroness's wall. There she collapsed on the lawn, which was covered with a thin layer of silvery frost.

My father, standing at the tall window in his studio where he painted his stained glass, had seen Cornélie escape. Wishing to save me heartbreak, he once more alerted all his workmen, who dragged out ladders and prepared to scale the baroness's wall. She was called and warned of the impending invasion. She was most gracious. "Your daughter must be my grandson's age," she said. "She must come for tea one day."

I ran to tell Mieke this news, bragging a little at my triumph, yet the prospect filled me with shyness. Not only would the formality of the strange house be intimidating, but I knew no boys at all. The Catholic hierarchy of Roermond was such that schools, swimming pools, and tennis clubs as well as street games were totally segregated. If a boy was seen bicycling with a girl, a priest would warn their parents that a dangerous relationship was developing. At home there were only Sylvia and I, and though Mieke had an older brother who had been present at Sunday dinners, I blushed whenever he said a word to me. Male and female children led separate lives. Only the baroness could get away with breaking the rule.

On Mardi Gras she gave a masquerade party for her grandson and fortunately invited not only me, but Mieke, the children of the Chinese doctor, both boys and girls, and even my sister. "But Sylvia is too young," I objected. "She will cry. She will have to go to the bathroom. Must she?" Sylvia was by then eight years old and perfectly capable of taking care of herself. She looked irresistible in a black cat costume with a velvet tail, but I felt that her impish presence would detract from my romantic entrance at the party. My own costume was a ballerina's tutu, ballerinas being exotic in those days when ballet classes were unheard of in the provinces. With its tight waist, fluffy skirt, and a wreath of flowers in my bobbed hair, I felt graceful and light. Mieke, dressed as Red Riding Hood, led us around the corner.

In carnival season the streets were so full of excitement and music that everything seemed to dance. The hazy, gray March sky weighed delicately on the chimney tops and enveloped the town as if to separate it from the too vast possibilities of the rest of the world. On the market square stood a dance tent with colored light bulbs, painted murals, and red velvet armchairs. There Anna, the maid, danced at night with her young man, which meant we would be dining on cold meat for a week. There children could ride the merry-go-round or buy *poffertjes,* round doughnuts made in vast copper pots.

Mieke now pulled the brass bell of the imposing house. The butler took our coats and we followed him through halls with many doors to a drawing room with gilt mirrors on the walls and long velvet curtains at the windows. The children of the Chinese doctor stood giggling in a cluster in one corner, all five of them dressed as one dragon. They faced a pale boy with lank blond hair who wore a velvet suit with a lace collar and a crown. He stood staring at us with aloof superiority while the dragon, wiggling and bobbing, shouted, "I'm Carla, I'm Marli, I'm Josje, I'm Frans, I'm Dolf." Then, snorting and hissing, it dissolved in hysterics and started all over again but in reverse, "I'm Dolf, I'm Frans, I'm Josje . . ." Finally the door to the adjoining room was opened by the butler onto a table full of delicacies, and the dragon children abandoned their disguise to crowd with shameless greediness around the table. If it hadn't been for their irrepressible high spirits, the gathering would have been awkward.

The baroness appeared briefly out of a side door and mumbled something benign, nodded, raised her lorgnette, and disappeared again. Marli filled her mouth with chocolates and put some in her pocket. She was Sylvia's age, and together they crawled under the tablecloth, meowing and scratching people's ankles, but our host was not amused. His name was Willem, he volunteered, then opened his mouth wide and let a huge fragile spit bubble grow out of it. None of us could blow one like it, which made him smile with satisfaction. "We shall play hide-and-seek in the dark," he said with the guttural accent of the North. "Follow me."

He led us through the carpeted halls up a wide staircase with carved railings. The landing was hung with hunting tapestries, the long hall lined with painted ancestors in shiny black frames, the doors closed. We entered the boy's room and when he switched on the light it threw the shadow of a Norman ship against the wall. The bed was covered with a baldachin, and green silk curtains enclosed it. Armies of tin soldiers marched in formation on the table, and above it hung a curved sword with a gilt-edged handle and an engraved blade.

The boy sat down on an armchair that looked like a throne, and we stood around him, gaping at all the splendor that was his. Since his crown kept slipping sideways, he held it with one hand as he explained the game. "I'll be *it*," he said, "and you go and hide. You can go all over the house, except in the kitchen or in my grandmother's living room. I'll count to a hundred. Then I'll come and look for you. The last one found wins." Curious, impatient to explore the mysterious rooms and luxuries of this house, we were all about to disperse when he added, "One of you has to keep me company. Who will it be?" We eyed each other, ill at ease and perplexed. Mieke, the oldest, who looked like a nanny in her red cape, stepped forward and was about to volunteer when the boy smiled slyly at me. "How about you?" he said. "You're my size." The others all left at once. I stood there in my sleeveless dancer's costume, shivering. "Why don't you sit down?" the boy said and stared at the ceiling, his crown falling off his head. His hands were thin and his voice was high and squeaky. There was a bluish pallor to his face. I sat down awkwardly on the edge of a second throne next to the bed and looked at my feet in their pink slippers for a long time. Feeling his eyes on me, I noticed that he was blowing another of his shimmering bubbles. He popped it and said, "We can count to a hundred as slowly as we want. We'll make them wait all afternoon in the dark." Then a clever, queer smile crept over his face, showing his pointed teeth. He got up and took my hand. His was wet and hot, smaller than mine. He drew me toward him till I felt his breath on my neck. "I have to go home now," I said and ran out of the room. Doors closed quickly, shadows moved in the dark. The stairs creaked. "Sylvia," I cried. "It's time to go home. Come!"

She appeared from behind the tapestry. "What do you mean?" she said. "He hasn't counted to a hundred yet." I grabbed her hand and pinched it, dragging her down the stairs. The butler met us in the hall and I asked for our coats. "We don't have to go yet," whined Sylvia. "It was just beginning to be fun." In the streets she shook me off and sulked. "It's not fair. You always spoil everything. The game had only just begun."

"That was no game at all," I said. "He was tricking us." But I could not explain my fear to my mother, nor even to myself, and in the end had to agree with them all that I was hopeless and had completely botched my introduction to society. Bonne Maman, especially, found me a ridiculous failure. "Artists," she said, "should feel inferior to no one!"

5
A SPECIAL CASE

Black and white was my world at convent school, the colors of suffering and purity. Perhaps this was a necessary apprenticeship—a black and white checkerboard world where everything was either one or the other, shadow or light, good or evil, allowed or forbidden, all other colors part of a banished childhood. Black the garments of the nuns sliding through white corridors, black my dress, white the round collar at my neck, black the priest's robe, white his lace surplice and dazzlingly white his cloak at elevation, black the confessional, and white the Host. The nuns' faces, framed in white and edged with black against the white background of the walls, seemed to burn like candle flames, and at times their black silhouettes were outlined by an astonishing electric halo. Squinting at them as they sat motionless in their supervision of us, I could see the halo of sainthood around the ones I loved and I suppressed it around those I feared.

There was one, a poor, harsh soul with the face of a dog. She taught us catechism and tried to communicate to us her terrifying enthusiasm for death. When describing the beauties of a nun's last hours surrounded by her singing sisters, her eyes burned with longing in her prominent skull. At bedtime she read us descriptions of the wars in Spain and China and showed us photographs of dying children shot down in village streets. This could happen to us. We must be prepared!

I did not want to die, only to survive these convent days and emerge once more into a world of color. I opened my desk during study hall and on my calendar I crossed out each day wasted in misery. In this desk, too, I hid a book with colored illustrations by Edy Legrand — landscapes full of Chinese pagodas, exotic birds, tall sailing ships, and people dressed in velvet covered with jewels. This was an antidote to the book I had been given to read during Lent, a life of blessed Guy de Fontgallant, who died angelically without a single complaint at the age of twelve. My twelfth birthday was approaching!

The dog-faced nun, sitting high up on her desk as on a throne, clacked her little bell and in her toneless voice called my name. "What are you doing with your desk open?" Blushing, I slammed down the lid and looked up into black and white. I dipped my pen hastily into an inkwell choked with scraps of paper and copied another Latin verb, peering through the haze of tears that dampened my glasses.

This same nun, no doubt unjustly overworked, loomed over us in the refectory, where we sat at long white tables, our chairs scraping the stone floor. No sooner was grace said than three hundred hands reached for the piles of buttered bread, sometimes tearing the slices in two. These piles were fresh on the top but stale toward the bottom. The French girls ate the bread with their hands, smacking their lips; the Dutch girls cut the slices on their plates into tiny geometric strips, which they daintily lifted to their mouths with forks. But though they pretended great refinement in their eating habits, the Dutch boarders were taller and rougher than the small-boned French girls, whose gentler ways were a revelation to me.

During Lent no jam was served and the dry bread stuck in my throat, tasting of tears. Lunch, the main meal of the day, was an obstacle that grew daily more insurmountable. It varied from slices of beef cooked leather hard and sometimes iridescent with an unexplainable green sheen, to sausage swimming in fat served with a puree of kale and potatoes, to dried cod. For dessert there were apples that grew more shriveled as winter wore on. The pink jello with fruit inside, a Sunday treat, looked deceptively pretty in color.

My stomach, pinched by the uncomfortable garter belt holding up my thick cotton stockings, always hurt. Though uncomplaining, I was stubborn. It began with the cod, hard and yellow at the edges. I refused to eat it, and when everyone filed out to the playground I was kept seated in front of my plate. The dog-faced nun begged and threatened, but to no avail. I sat motionless, speechless, and fully aware of the fact that my refusal to eat filled me with power. When recreation was over, the plate was removed but carefully preserved and served up again at teatime and supper.

At bedtime, as I sat still determined in front of the cold meal, it became evident that I had won the battle of wills. The nun lost her patience and slapped me. Precisely at that moment Mother Superior entered the refectory and dismissed her with quiet severity. She herself sat down and gently began to feed me forkful by forkful, as if I were a small child, and, suddenly pacified, I ate. The unfortunate dog-faced nun remained imprisoned behind the cloister walls for several weeks, and I kept my sense of triumph to myself. But during those sessions when our characters were publicly discussed, our faults pointed out and remedies suggested, I understood that by not advertising my sin of pride I could be accused of hypocrisy as well.

It was Mother Superior's personality that had won me over. A handsome woman, she could only be described as an ideal of aristocracy: just, gentle, remarkably strong, and always in control of herself and situations. Her hands never moved, her back was always straight, her voice was melo-dious, and the dark eyes in her pale face glowed with a velvet warmth that could be tender as well as severe. In the feudal structure of this female community, she was our queen, remote and apparently without weakness. If I chanced upon her while wandering through the echoing halls of the convent, usually during my endless comings and goings to the bathroom, I would flatten myself against the wall. Then the curtsey that was due to all the nuns we encountered was not the usual mere flexing of the knee but a ceremonious bow. The mere rustle of her garments, the tinkling of her rosary, and the creaking of her firmly laced boots as she swept by made my heart beat faster. Had she noticed me dawdling by the reproductions of Alma Tad-ema's paintings or lingering by the window from which one could look down on the garden descending to the banks of the Rhine? To be allowed to go to the bathroom only by permission confused me, and I invariably used this excuse to escape from study hall, to feel free and unobserved, so that when I actually needed to go I had used up all my permissions and spent hours in a panic, wiggling in my chair, suppressing the need.

It came to Mother Superior's attention that I was heard weeping every night in my bed. It was true that as soon as I was allowed to close the white curtains that separated me from the twenty other girls in the dormitory, I indulged in rather melodramatic sobbing. One morning she sum-moned me to her office. She did not remain behind her forbidding desk but pulled back her chair and held out her arms.

"Come here. Sit on my lap," she said. Surprised, I perched awkwardly on her knee. With inexperienced motherliness she put her arms around me, but her starched bib got in the way.

"They tell me you cry at night. Are you not happy here?" I shrugged and said nothing. She caressed my hair and seemed puzzled. She did not smell of sour milk and white bread like the other nuns. Though I was one of the youngest boarders in the school, I was getting too big and heavy to sit on anyone's lap and realized that I was crushing a leg made of flesh and bone even though swathed in black drapery.

"I'll tell you what we'll do. Since you are a special case, coming from an unusual background, we'll let you spend an hour every day alone in the garden with your sketchbook while the others are at study period."

And so, once more committing the sin of hypocrisy, I kept carefully hidden my pride at being considered a special case. I began to spend study hour wandering sedately through the park, down to the river on which barges passed, whole families waving at me from the deck. In the vegetable gardens, cloistered nuns emerged into the light of day: kitchen and laundry nuns and old sick ones with mustaches, pale like the insects one finds under stones. They called me sweet, silly names and looked at my drawings, which, to please them, were usually of madonnas and angels. But though I enjoyed my privilege, I still cried at night and read *The Little Princess* with a flashlight under the covers.

Then one day Mother Superior told me that my father was coming for a visit. He had written her to announce his arrival a week ahead and had sent her some photographs of the altar he had made for a church in Arnhem. This was the height of my father's baroque period. He had invented a new medium he called glass mural, with which he was covering all manner of surfaces, walls, and picture frames

as well as our dining room table and a monumental double
bed in which he and Mother looked rather uncomfortable.
Among the arabesques on its baldachin and side tables,
mermaids and cupids cavorted on mirrored glass. Now the
altar in Arnhem was adorned in the same style. The photographs were passed around among the students. Mother
Superior gave a short lecture on Father's accomplishments,
and only the nun who taught us art dared to comment
discreetly, "I wonder if it's in very good taste?"

Since Father had by then attained the height of success, I
never questioned his excellence, and besides, my school-
mates now eyed me with interest. Suddenly I was offered
candies and talked to by the "elder" girls.

"Will he take you out to eat pastries? Can I come too?"
they asked me. On the calendar inside my desk I circled the
day of his visit with red pencil and counted the hours.
Finally the moment came when I was called out of study
hall, told to put on a clean white collar and go to the *parloir*.
It seemed significant that in a convent there should be a
room specially set aside in which to converse, since this was
something we were not allowed to do anywhere else. During recreation we played strenuous, organized games, and
in class we were only expected to answer questions. Yet as I
approached the parlor full of potted palms, red upholstery,
and portraits of the founding mothers of the *Chanoinesses
de Saint Augustin,* I felt myself growing utterly tongue-tied.
I stood in the long corridor by the umbrella stand on the
red strip of carpet in the pink and yellow light streaming
through the colored glass window over the front entrance.
There I listened to the voices of Father and Mother Superior, who were engaged in animated conversation behind
closed doors.

"I do not see any reason why religious art should be cold
and stylized. Splendor and gaiety are an important part of
worship."

"Why, certainly, *Maître* Nicolas, I quite agree with you. And this technique of glass mural, it must have great possibilities?"

"Opaque, you see, yet with all the liveliness of glass, so that one can have entire walls made of it, to be decorated at will. I foresee its use in modern architecture on a large scale."

"How interesting," she murmured. I stood motionless on one leg while the clock in the hall ticked away and Father talked. The doorkeeper sister came by with her keys and looked at me.

"Is Mother Superior still in the *parloir?*" I nodded. She raised one eyebrow and went away again, gliding through the long corridor like a bat, back to the *clôture*, the mysterious door to the cloister where no students had ever been.

The familiar voice holding forth soothed me. How many hours of my life had I spent being lulled by it, not really listening but attentive, respectful? I had not yet learned to pose the questions about history, art, etymology, and politics that launched my father on his monologues. Mother Superior excelled at it, and I realized that for all her aloofness, her technique was no different from that of the worldlier women who courted him. Three-quarters of an hour went by as I sat on the radiator outside the cozy seclusion of the parlor. Finally the door flew open and Father burst out in a flurry, followed by Mother Superior, saying, "Where could the child be?" They discovered me with some embarrassment.

"Why didn't you knock on the door, *fifille?*" Mother Superior caressed my hair with apologetic tenderness. Father looked at his watch, saying, "My, my. We'll have to hurry. I haven't much time left."

He did drive me to a tearoom then, commenting on the charms of this "truly cultivated great lady" and congratulating himself for having put me in her charge. "You are very lucky," he said, and I did not contradict him. As I stuffed myself with éclairs and napoleons he peered out of the window while I kept a sullen silence. How could I explain to him that the charms of Mother Superior did not quite equal those of home?

6
MY FRIEND RENÉE

What a terrible thing first friendship is, like leaving one's body to move into another. Inevitably the moment would come when I would discover that my friend Renée no longer conformed to the ideal I had thought she was, and I would have to shrink back into myself, stand on my own two feet, reinhabit my own skin. But for a while I loved her the way it is not possible ever to love again.

Like me, she was a boarder at the convent, a girl with pale, sweaty skin and very dark eyes. I first perceived her sitting in the back of study hall, her arms draped about a stick held behind her back. In a certain sense she was crucified but didn't seem to mind, perhaps because the books she studied with great attention had better pictures in them than mine, for she was a class ahead of me.

"Why are you crucified?" I asked her. She had grown crooked from playing the violin, she said. I imagined her fiddling gypsy tunes standing on one leg, her lank, greasy hair falling over her face. She always stood on one leg, perhaps because of the crooked spine. My spine had a "double scoliosis" too, I said. Besides, my feet were flat and I had bow legs. Every day I had to crawl about the gym for half an hour on all fours, then walk on my insteps for another ten minutes according to the latest method of corrective gymnastics. The bow legs could not be cured. I had been told by an orthopedic nurse that they would have to be broken in a thousand pieces, then set straight again.

I bragged about all this to Renée, even though I was desperately sad to have a crooked body at the age of twelve. Still, Renée did not seem to mind. She knew that she would become what she wanted to be. "I shall be an aristocrat," she announced, and tied her apron strings very tight so as to have a small waist. During recreation she walked with her hands up in the air so they would grow white. Her pride intimidated me; it was her imagination that I admired, for it reminded me of my Uncle Eric.

Renée was French. She twisted her mouth and her lips moved fast. She even spat a little when she spoke. Her mother came from the Pays Basque, where her family lived in a medieval castle. This was a country of smuggling bandits who crossed secret mountain passes to Spain in the night, a wild and proud people of unknown origin. Her father claimed descent from Chateaubriand, Renée's idol, who grew up in an even grander and gloomier castle and whose romantic tomb overlooks the windswept rocky shore of Brittany.

Renée gave me Loti's *Ramuntcho* to read and taught me the ballad of Jean Renaud, a medieval knight who came back from war carrying his guts in his hands. When he died, his pregnant wife ordered the earth to open and swallow her with his child so she might join Renaud, her king. Ramuntcho, Renaud, Renée—was it not the same name? My friend's eyes flashed, her mouth twisted with passion as the earth seemed to gape beneath her feet, but no sooner had her throaty voice ceased singing than a slight smile played at the corners of her mouth. She could tell by my sigh of concentration that I was enthralled.

Renée was an admirer of the famous bluestockings who ruled eighteenth-century Paris with their salons, and she emulated the more romantic nineteenth-century heroines as well. During recreation she lay stretched out on two chairs, being now "La Récamier," the famous beauty whose hand Napoleon kissed, now Madame de Staël, now George Sand smoking a cigar dressed as a man or the blind Madame du Deffand in her bonnet. We were told to court her and to make brilliant conversation, but though Renée displayed a convincing *esprit,* that truly Gallic form of literary wit, our repartee was rather slow. Then I remembered that Madame du Deffand had had a famous rival, her secretary, Mademoiselle de L'Espinasse, who stole all her admirers. I lay down myself on two other chairs and established a court of my own, waving my hands and spouting refined nonsense. Soon I, too, was surrounded by an audience. Madame du Deffand imperiously fired me as her secretary but I rose in her esteem. From then on I was enrolled as a worthy partner in Renée's extravagant games.

On the playground we were expected to play energetic ball games at which the athletic Dutch girls excelled. Renée, too, threw a mean ball, gritting her teeth and frowning angrily. She would skip about like a sparrow on her spindly legs, and when a chance came to escape supervision, would draw me along the shady paths of the park.

"Let's play Napoleon," she suggested. I felt at a disadvantage, for obviously in this game she would be the hero.

"You can be Murat," she explained. "Here we are in Egypt after the Victory of the Pyramids." Her hand slipped into her apron and, exhausted, she leaned on my shoulder and declaimed, obviously quoting, "From the heights of these monuments forty centuries look down on us."

"Who was Murat?" I asked. Impatiently Renée instructed me, but I was not satisfied.

"I'll tell you what," I said. "I'll be William of Orange."

She looked puzzled. "Do you mean the medieval knight?"

"No, the leader of the Dutch rebellion in 1572, the founder of our nation."

When I had told her about my hero, she agreed that he would be a worthy rival. The fact that William and Napoleon had lived three centuries apart did not bother us. We chose our troops on the playground, planned strategy, stalked each other through the rhododendron bushes, and met in a decisive battle, at the end of which Napoleon and William engaged in mortal combat. After some brilliant swordplay I realized to my horror that I had wounded my worthy opponent. He stumbled and slowly collapsed on the mossy banks, clutching his heart, and looked up at me with a resigned and noble love.

"*Adieu*, friend, enemy. You have won a rightful victory. Be generous with my soldiers. Europe is yours, but remember that France is its heart. As for my death, I forgive you."

These moving words brought tears to the eyes of our audience, which included several nuns gathered about us. Obviously, it was Renée who had won the game. The next time we played it was on condition that it would be my turn to die and make the farewell speech, but as I sank down among the ferns and uttered my last breath I heard Napoleon, standing over me, deliver a glowing eulogy to the assembled armies. With three other soldiers, she picked me up and they carried me on their shoulders in a stately procession to my final rest. Once more Renée had outdone me in theatrical imagination.

The nuns watched our friendship develop with prurient interest. We were suddenly chosen to perform together at all the literary and musical soirées given in honor of visiting mother superiors. Renée was the boy St. John who came to visit baby Jesus and I was the Virgin Mary. "Ah, there you are, you charming mischief with bushy hair like ears of rye," I sang, cradling a doll in my arms. Another time we were two birds to whom Saint Francis had taught a prayer. "God of little birds," we declaimed in unison, "who to make us lighter put air in our bones . . ."

We were flowers and pine trees, we wore beehives on our heads, we did an idiotic little skipping dance in matching elf costumes with antennae and pointed wings, choreography not being a strong subject in convents. We were also Christopher Robin and Winnie the Pooh and had great difficulty pronouncing *th* and the other strange breezy noises of the English language.

When we all wrote compositions on "the house of our dreams," the two winning efforts, copied in a fair hand in the Honor Book, were Renée's and mine. Hers described a dark Gothic castle with thick walls, a moat, a ghost with rattling chains and, to cheer things up, geraniums in the window boxes. My dream house was a farm by the sea with a thatched roof, a horse in the meadow, a garden full of roses, and a playpen with a baby in it. It was after this triumph that we confided to each other our ambition to become writers.

One day we had a fight, but I can't remember what it was about. Perhaps, as happens in such possessive relationships, we simply decided not to talk to each other for a while, to state our independence. Was it possible to live separate lives? Who would be the first to break down? We went about our school days ignoring each other, taking up rival friendships, and engaging in unnaturally gay conversation and loud laughter within each other's earshot.

Our behavior upset the entire community. "Did you quarrel?" the older girls inquired. "Don't you like Renée anymore?"

"Who, Renée? She's all right," I shrugged coolly. There was a trace of mockery in Renée's eyes as she walked by, flaunting a train of new admirers. The nuns, too, were worried.

"What's going on between those two?" I heard them ask each other. Finally I was summoned by Mother Superior.

"Who started it?" she probed. "What happened?"

Once more I felt power, the power to disturb all these women's idea of a passionate friendship. Perhaps Renée and I were really accomplices in a secret plot, feigning enmity to tease them, playing another elaborate game. But, stubborn, I was determined not to be the first to give in, so it was Renée who made the opening move. She did this grandly, generously. We looked at each other and laughed, relieved. "Didn't we have them all worried, though? But after all, what business was it of theirs?"

Together we rebelled against our imprisonment in the convent and shared our homesickness, describing to each other what we most missed, namely, our mothers — both, according to us, women of extraordinary beauty and strange, exotic charm. "She is not the obvious kind," I said, "but sophisticated, original, artistic. Her nose is quite long and a bit crooked and her front teeth overlap. She wears her hair in a bun in the nape of the neck."

"So does my mother!" exclaimed Renée, and described a cape and hat her mother wore made of yellow and brown brocade with little balls dangling around the edge. This garment fascinated me, and Renée wrote her mother to be sure to wear it when she came for a spring visit. But when I finally met Renée's mother, I was disappointed. She was a small, dry-skinned woman, rather mousy. Her hair was pinned back in a tight little knot, not a romantic Spanish chignon, and the toque with all those wobbly balls around the edge looked silly and dowdy on her head. No doubt my mother was a more genuine beauty, but this triumph gave me little pleasure. I longed for Renée to be invincible, superior, a heroine I could count on. When I discovered that she had no more daring than I, it was a great disappointment.

This happened at the end of a long game we played, called Escape, during the last spring we were together in the convent. I described our old farmhouse by the sea where my family had spent the vacation at Easter time, when it was still cold and windy. It had a special appeal then — the smell of water, the frogs' eggs in the ditches, the dampness in the house and sheets, the lambs and calves bleating on the polders, the sky in a constant turmoil of clouds sweeping by. She suggested we run away and go there. The idea filled us with excitement. We spent hours discussing details: money, the train ride to Amsterdam, the change at Alkmaar, where, smelling the sea, we would get on the bus. We would ask the postmaster for the key or break into the house and tell no one of our presence. And how would we escape from the convent? It would be in the night. I would climb out of my window in the dormitory and creep to Renée's room along the wide gutter that surrounded the roof. This private room, which she shared with her sister, was in a wing of the building near the river. We would tear up our sheets and tie them together, then slide down them to the ground. We would ask a passing barge to take us as far as the next town.

Weeks went by as we planned our escape. The nuns, relieved to see us reconciled, suspected nothing but viewed us with tender indulgence. Finally we set the date, the hour, and began smuggling food out of the refectory for provisions. "Tonight!" whispered Renée solemnly. "Knock three times on the windowpane." We clasped hands with beating hearts.

But as soon as I lay down in my bed I knew I would never dare creep along the gutter and that I was, furthermore, incapable of staying awake till midnight. I fell asleep, disappointed in myself, and the next day met Renée as if nothing were meant to have happened. She never mentioned my failure to appear and I was ashamed of her evasiveness even more than of mine. This, too, had been merely a game after all. So the school year ended and we parted, almost relieved. Our unemotional farewells were a disappointment to the nuns.

I never saw Renée again, but just before leaving for the United States, in the autumn of 1939, I received a letter from her. The paper was blue, the handwriting hasty, passionate. Drawings of Marianne with her republican flag as well as the royalist lily were scribbled around the edges.

"As you know, we are now at war. I must tell you that it almost makes me happy for:

> Divided in peace,
> United in suffering,
> The inequality of the French
> Is leveled in misfortune.

But most of all, you better than anyone know that I can only accept death on the battlefield."

That is where I buried Renée, in that blue letter, under her drawing of a little mound on which were planted a cross and the tricolored flag. Though no doubt she lives on somewhere, a suburban housewife in Versailles wearing a hat with a fringe of little balls, my first heroine personified the spirit of resistance and must be buried during that last war, when patriotism still had a meaning.

7
THE FIFTH WHEEL

She ate her chicken with jam, her ham with pineapple slices. Her nose was sharp and long as a blade, her forehead high and knobby, her tongue too big for her mouth so that she held onto it with her teeth. Her long hair was always flapping against her nose like a sail against a mast. She was the color of a wet beach on a gray day and spoke very slowly in a voice that was always on the verge of laughter, undulating in the higher register. She played Liszt with too much pedal and kept her fingernails so long that one heard them rap the piano keys. These narrow hands, constantly tucking her limp hair behind an ear, were covered with very good rings. The servants called her Freule, a title of aristocracy, and though she had a Dutch name she had spent most of her life in the United States, so she was therefore our first American.

I was twelve when she joined our family circle. Constantly drawing attention to the oddities of her person, she enjoyed nothing better than being laughed at, or with, or about, and this generosity was irresistible. Yet it was with slight mistrust that I received this young woman, whom we had nicknamed Ficelle, into our midst. At an age when children are conformists, I found her eccentricities embarrassing. The costume she ordered from our local tailor was a skirt of half purple, half magenta with a matching cape and peaked hat. So attired, she would ride into town on a yellow racing bike, making a flashy contrast to the Dutch on their conservative black vehicles with their high, dignified handlebars.

Her presence in our midst caused me another, nameless malaise. I could not attribute to her an official title or function in our family. Father jokingly called her now our governess, now his assistant, now part of his harem. When my parents were invited to a masquerade ball in Brussels, Father dressed as a vegetable, Mother was sheathed in white petals, and Ficelle went along as a dandelion in a yellow dress swathed in clouds of spun glass. This glass, it seems, got in everyone's eyes, hands, and mouth, so that Ficelle found herself without partners for the entire evening.

No longer was the house pregnant with the rather melancholy silence of private occupations. The days were filled with group activities from which we, the children, were no longer excluded. Ficelle posed while we drew her, dressed in turbans, tassels, nothing, paper bags, or wet sheets, which, she insisted, took on exactly the same folds as the garments of Greek statues. For her, the result of this experiment was a bout with pneumonia. We also played charades or took turns dancing for each other in the proscenium arch formed by the double doors between the studio and the dining room. Lamps laid on the floor were the floodlights, and to a record of Haydn's German dances we were now rabbits, now Siamese twins (with two legs in one stocking), now the dying swan, while my father tottered about like a majestic bear. She had a passion for interior decorating, and covered the bureaus and woodwork with minute paintings of sea horses and exotic fish. Glass Christmas tree balls hung in clusters from the ceiling.

At the least suspicion of sun she dragged us to the roof, where we lay bathing in the nude, suffocating in the damp heat, our embarrassed modesty gradually succumbing to Ficelle's matter-of-factness. Our anatomies were discussed freely. Her left breast, slightly larger than the right, was called Pavnusse, for some reason. My knees were knobby but interesting. My mother had a large round beauty spot on her back that was compared to a Droste milk chocolate pastille.

Ficelle was also addicted to architectural plans. Drawings for a projected house were fussed over. Three arches? Two arches? An indoor swimming pool? Should the front door be American colonial? Then building was suddenly abandoned and we must rush to an outlying village where she had discovered the ideal manor house with a moat and a ballroom. Its walls were covered with frescoes done in blue silhouette, but this ballroom was used by the farmer to store his grain, and chickens walked up and down the stairs. It was lovely, we all agreed, and for a while it was called "Ficelle's House." She was asked to be the godmother of the farmer's tenth child. Although she bicycled to "her house" regularly, she never actually moved out of our ménage.

How different life was suddenly. There was a constant excitement in the air. Father whistled and beamed. Mother, until then lonely and foreign, now had a constant companion who understood her and was just as different from the other women of the town. We began to travel in caravan. The soothing routine of holidays in the old farmhouse by the North Sea was abandoned for Christmas in Mégève, Easter in Ostend, summer in the South of France where mother's sister, Maria Huxley, lent us her home. We females became a family block, a frivolous chorus that, by contrast, enhanced the masculinity of Father's figure. To keep us in line, tyranny was practically forced upon him. But instead of trembling at his tantrums, we conspirators now tittered behind his back. Besides, Ficelle could soothe him with a word, tame him with a caress. Mother seemed grateful at first. We waited by the banks of the Loire while he lay napping under a tree, a newspaper over his face, groaning at the discomfort of insects and the hard ground. We held our breath when, in a hairpin curve on a road through Champagne, he stopped the car in the middle of the road and announced he would never move again. At the edge of the precipice, hanging over the dazzling prospect of vine-yards, he cried out, "I don't care if we all get killed. This is just too beautiful!"

We must have been a nuisance. Whenever he packed the car with easel, oils, and canvas to paint a long-coveted view in the ripening light of the afternoon, the four of us would jump in too with our own drawing boards, pads, and watercolors. The view he had chosen was invariably obstructed by his female entourage, and the silence of the Alpes Maritimes destroyed by songs and complaints. "I need some white! My water fell down . . . Who has my eraser? I'm sitting on an anthill!" Upon returning home we compared our work. My sister's and mine was considered original and precocious, but the Master's efforts were routinely ignored.

The summer was drawing to a close. I had hoped to meet Aunt Maria and her husband, about whom I had heard so much, but they had left the previous year for the United States. In the cafés of Saint-Tropez, we met degenerate English poets with pet praying mantises who drank absinthe. We sipped Pam Pam, the bottled juice of a then-exotic fruit called *pamplemousse*, or grapefruit. One evening, sitting on a terrace by a harbor, we dined on aioli in the company of a virile young Dutchman. He was blond and blue-eyed and I watched him with a first girlish thrill. Suddenly he began to shout about heaven knows what, and jumping to his feet, raised his right arm and cried, *"Heil Hitler!"* Ficelle took my sister and me firmly by the hand and dragged us away, muttering, "How disgusting. In front of children!" I concluded that I had been exposed to a dirty joke. Yet Ficelle's prudishness was puzzling because it was out of character. Subdued, she led us along the docks, among fishing boats and drying nets. We watched the harbor lights reflected in the water and listened to the sound of *valses musettes* drifting out of the cafés.

The next day, Father decided it was time to go home. "We don't want to be caught in France if something happens." He meant war, though I didn't know it then. And so the car was packed with everyone's masterpieces, leaving very little room for us. We drove through Marseilles, where Mother and Ficelle refused to be rushed. "We must see the fish markets," they insisted, and wandered among the glistening baskets of seafood and the shouting vendors, who slapped their fish on wooden counters to carve them up. Mother's bare brown feet in sandals picked their way elegantly through the slimy muck. Nauseated by the smell, we followed but refused to eat the raw mussels held out to us by a smiling walrus of a fisherman. Greedily, mother sucked at the black shells, and Ficelle, pointing at two huge, desiccated blowfish mummies hung like Chinese lanterns on the fish stall, cried, "Ooh, I want them, I want them!" She bargained and walked off, daintily swinging the black, wrinkled fish balloons, their buckteeth grinning, and hung them from the ceiling of the car.

On the road to Avignon, Mother began to writhe with a pain in her stomach. Sitting next to Father on the front seat, her head twisted and turned while she gasped and moaned softly. We held our breath and listened to her suffer as the wheels swallowed the road ahead. Then she fell over and Father abruptly stopped the car, exclaiming, *"Elle est morte!* She's dead!"

In a panic Sylvia and I ran away from the car, clinging to each other, under the dreadful noonday sun of the Midi, in a field by a roadside a thousand miles from home, more alone than we would ever be again.

Mother turned out not to be dead, only poisoned by the mussels. We were called back to the car and drove on to Avignon, where she was put to bed. For dinner we ate *tourte aux épinards,* a gastronomical consolation for emotional crisis, but afterward Father sat somberly listening to the radio in the hotel lobby, spellbound by the horrid voice of Hitler shouting at the world.

That night it took a lot of doing for Ficelle to cheer him up. Mother lay in a darkened room with a high fever. By the time we reached home, she had recovered her health but she looked frail and abandoned and seemed restless. She now began to question Ficelle about America. "I told you I was unhappy there. I never want to go back," Ficelle answered. Perhaps that was precisely why Mother set her mind on going there, a continent without Hitler or Ficelle who, though her best friend, was nevertheless becoming a fifth wheel in our family.

But Ficelle was already planning our next holiday. That winter we would go skiing in Austria, she decided. The entertainments she invented were irresistible. She had become so much a part of our household that we could no longer imagine doing anything without her.

That autumn, storms brewed in the garden, doors slammed suddenly, Father's voice rose in odd outbursts of excitement, Ficelle's laughter seemed forced, and Mother remained oppressively silent. One evening she announced unexpectedly that she was leaving for Paris. "But why?" I asked. "We only just came back." She did not answer me; she was too preoccupied to address any of us. Why Paris, I wondered, that evil, corrupt city—as I had been told by priests and nuns—where my dangerous Aunt Jeanne lived? On a beautiful evening, I clung to Mother as we drove to the station. When we had waved good-bye to her small, unsmiling figure, I began to cry. Father, upset and puzzled, tried to console me in his own oblique way. He made a detour along a dirt road down by the river.

This river world was a deep, green place through which one zigzagged on tiny ferries. Here villages clung to chapels dating back to the fourth century, dedicated to pagan saints whose bones, fingers, heads, or entire bodies were set in gold reliquaries encrusted with jewels and preserved in damp crypts below the churches. Brick farms squatted somberly under vast roofs, their shutters and doors painted in geometric patterns. From every streetcorner or lonely crossroad, crucifixes and saints reached out their pleading arms. But the village Father showed me now was cheerful, entirely whitewashed, surrounded by orchards. The people sat on their doorsteps and, as we passed, saluted with a peaceful "Evening." Children stared at us shyly, suspending their games. The last rays of the sun were a gently blue benison. The faces of the people were more refined, less earthy, than in other villages. The place seemed remote, elegant, enchanted.

Father said, "The history of this village is very interesting. For centuries it has been a tradition for well-to-do girls from the cities to bring their illegitimate children here to be brought up by the farmer's wives."

"What are illegitimate children?"

Father muttered something under his breath at my ignorance. His explanation was unsatisfactory ("Children without fathers"), and the beauty of the village was spoiled somewhat by the uneasiness I felt whenever life turned out to differ from the way I had been taught it must be.

"Let's go home," I said crossly. "After all, I'm not illegitimate!" which made him laugh.

* * *

The room Sylvia and I shared adjoined a loft that had been transformed into Father's studio, one wall covered by a drawing board. Here he would stand until late into the night on his movable ladder to cover the paper with silhouettes of saints, angels, and devils, as if creating huge ecclesiastical funny papers.

On other nights, Mother and Ficelle sat there, reclining on the sofa after dinner, murmuring about feminine things such as clothes, curtains, children, and servants, now and then looking up at their hero, whom Mother called Yoopee and Ficelle called Pooh Bear. But this evening I knew him to be alone and was therefore surprised to hear his voice in a long monologue addressed to his Little String. He was talking to her on the phone in embarrassing baby talk. Guiltily, I held my breath and listened behind the door.

"Why, yes, Ficelle. . . . Why of course you must come with your Pooh Bear. We'll spend the night in Amsterdam together." The sinking feeling, the darkness of danger, drowned me then like a tide from far back, but it was not until Mother's fur coat was mentioned that my anger felt justified. It was made of curly, undyed lamb and when she wore it she looked precious, gentle, and slightly pampered. It was her great luxury. I heard Father say, "The white fur?" No, I don't think she took it. You'd like it? All right, I'll bring it along."

Blind with rage, I stepped into the studio and blurted, "Why does 'she' need Mother's fur coat?" I had called Ficelle by that mean, vengeful pronoun *she*, which the maids used for Ficelle in the kitchen, thinking I would not understand, whenever she came to dinner unannounced or asked them to do her laundry, polish her shoes, make up a bed at the last minute, prepare a special oatmeal porridge, or fry her some thinly sliced bacon for breakfast. "Thinner! Thinner! In America they're mere slivers." They snickered about "she" whenever Ficelle appeared in sailor pants, a clinging Indian sari, or, suddenly coy, my convent school uniform, insisting upon wearing it when one of my father's clients, a Dominican abbot, came for dinner. Now, like them, I was talking about "she" as if about a resented intruder, and I blushed with shame. Still, fidgeting there in front of Father, unable to face his puzzled expression, I stood my ground.

"It's Mother's coat, not Ficelle's," I said. But words were never really necessary between us. He understood perfectly well what I meant.

The next day he did go to Amsterdam as planned, but Ficelle stayed with Sylvia and me. We had dinner alone at the table covered with pink mirrored glass on which Father had painted arabesques. There were candles in the candlesticks, "like in America," and Anna served us in her white apron. Since Bomma's death, our life-style had grown slightly pompous. Perhaps Ficelle, the aristocrat, had introduced this, or Father, more and more successful, had given in to a slight *folie des grandeurs*. Sylvia and I basked in this luxury and on this night I felt grateful to Ficelle. She looked me in the eye and said, "I was meant to go to Amsterdam today, but I chose to stay here so you two would not be alone."

"Ficelleke," cajoled Sylvia, nestling in her lap, tying her stringy hair in a knot below her chin. Ficelle pursed her lips, and with her long nose looked like an anteater. I burst out laughing, then caught myself, feeling disloyal to Mother, who was missing, who might not return.

But a few days later Mother did come home. She had made plans for me, she said. That winter I would go to school in Paris rather than to the convent. I would be staying with Aunt Jeanne, but though the excuse for her escape was to arrange for my future, I was certain she had also had a personal reason. No doubt she considered me, at thirteen, too old to be unaware of the ambiguous situation of their *ménage à trois*.

Jeanne, Ficelle—their names were French, foreign. There should be no harm in these names if I trusted the music in them. And so I did go to Paris, and the year after that our family did leave for America. But when we finally reached New York, Mother sat sad and alone in the dark bedroom of our apartment, reflecting on the difficult wrench out of Europe that she herself had largely engineered. Knowing that I had understood her dilemma, she said to me, "Isn't it stupid? Now all I can think of is that I have lost Ficelle, the best friend I ever had."

8
THE BODY

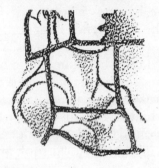

The Catholic puritanism of Roermond in those prewar days was aimed mostly at our bodies. They were supposed to be clothed so as not to arouse or distract. But in their art my parents celebrated the body nude or draped in flimsy shreds. Confused, I was caught in the middle and, during my early teens, became obsessed with health. A healthy and graceful body was surely a sign of being blessed by God.

The priests of our town hid their bodies behind black skirts. With houses of their own tended by housekeepers, they walked back and forth along the sidewalks in their flat, broad-brimmed hats or drove ladies' bicycles, the rear wheels protected by nets. The wide sashes around their waists were dashing, and in spite of the black camouflage they had a jaunty air of authority, of leading meaningful and productive lives. In a sense they owned the town. A bird's-eye view of Roermond would show it to be a conglomerate of church holdings: seminaries with vast walled

71

gardens, convents, the bishop's palace, the cathedral, the Church of Our Lady, the Chapel of the Miraculous Madonna-of-the-Sands, where pilgrims trekked beyond the city wall.

One of the gardens adjoining ours was that of Monsignor Thyssen. Walking on top of the brick wall had become my favorite pastime, and I surveyed those private heavens next to ours—the baroness's splendid, formal lawns and flowerbeds and the monsignor's garden, the size of a spacious city yard—with prurient curiosity. The latter contained a large bird cage housing exotic birds of all sorts. I had seen the monsignor enter it to feed them, standing in the midst of parakeets, thrushes, and rarer specimens, holding out his hands full of grain while they landed, chattering loudly on his head, shoulders, and arms.

I had been terrified of my own rook and was still frightened of all winged, fluttering things, with their feathery, restless motion, their fragile wings and tiny bones, their reptilian eyes and aggressive beaks. I thought the monsignor heroic and probably saintly, like Saint Francis, whom my father was always reproducing in his windows. A handsome, athletic man with a shock of white hair, he stood very still, whistling to his birds, absorbing their energy. He looked blissful, almost ecstatic, and I, hidden by the branches of the maple tree, felt indiscreet, as if I were watching something very private. There were of course flowers in the borders of his garden—tulips, roses, peonies, delphiniums, nasturtiums, dahlias—and on his way to and from the cage he would lean over them thoughtfully, his hands tucked into the broad sash around his middle.

One day in early summer a bright-colored pavilion was put up in his garden, one of those tents I had seen on the North Sea beaches that men use in trying to compromise with nature, half living in the open and yet not quite. It was the kind of thing the apostle Peter had in mind on the mountaintop where the transfiguration took place when he said, "Let us set up three tents, one for thee, one for Moses, and one for Elias." I knew gardens were contemplative places where people lost themselves in smells, colors, and airy sounds, and believed this one had something to do with God, for one of my favorite songs was an old Flemish one:

> Lord Jesus has a garden where
> sweet flowers grow.
> Therein I shall go picking, 'tis
> well done, I know.
> Therein one can hear angels sing
> and trumpets blow.
> Harps, clarinets, and violins
> and cymbals too.

But whatever did the monsignor plan to do under the yellow and white stripes of this tent?

I heard rumors in the place where all rumors gathered, the kitchen, brought back from the market by Anna along with the leeks and potatoes in her basket. "The monsignor's niece has consumption," she said. "She has come to die in his garden." Now terror of death filled me, as if death itself were contagious. Afraid of falling asleep forever, I no longer lay on my back with hands folded, for this was how the Duke and Duchess of Gelre lay on their tombs, with leverets at their feet, in the cathedral. Actually, this disease had haunted me for years. The baroness's grandson had a lung condition. And once when I was five a little girl my age called Magriet Cuypers had fallen off my swing and lain on the ground pale as a ghost.

She would not get up and I got cross with her. "You're showing off," I said, and refused to pay further attention, leaving her gasping in the grass.

The next thing I knew she had been sent away to spend years lying in a cast. "Tuberculosis of the spine," I was told, and I was certain it was my fault. Her mother had already died of consumption, and my own mother now disappeared for weeks at a time, "to take care of Magriet" somewhere in Amsterdam. Abandoned, guilty, jealous of Magriet, I had no choice but to accept Mother's absence as my due punishment.

After a bout of bronchitis when I was nine, I had myself been taken to a clinic in the country, in the midst of a pine forest, where I saw young people lying out in the cold air on balconies, freezing under light blankets beneath the dark, stiff pines. Torture, I thought. A doctor with a stethoscope knocked and poked at my lungs and back, drew signs in blue ink on my spine, and made X-rays of my ribs. All this was humiliating. I hated being stripped to my plain white ribbed-cotton underwear and, even worse, my bones.

I considered my body awkward and inadequate whenever it malfunctioned. Though the lungs inside passed inspection, the doctor said my back showed the "double scoliosis" of which I later bragged to Renée. My mother and I drove home in silence, and I suspect she felt she had botched me, making me doubly crooked. That night Anna scrubbed my back with pumice to remove the blue ink from the knobs of my spine, and for several years my body was left in peace.

Now there was this niece of Monsignor Thyssen's, who was dying, Anna said with her usual matter-of-factness, her relish of the morbid. I could hear voices in the garden, the gruff, hearty one of the monsignor and a lighter, airy one full of gaiety and laughter. From my post on the wall, camouflaged by branches, I never saw the body of the girl though in my imagination I had a distinct image of her, a beautiful, ethereal creature, with arms as thin as sticks and long red hair, brandishing a whip. The whip was an association I had made with the leading actress in a play I had seen the year before, an emaciated creature who had died shortly after the performance of a disease called T.B. She had played the part of a wicked queen, perhaps Jezebel, in a play by the classic Dutch author Vondel, and had brandished the whip with evil relish. Transferring the image of this villainess to that of the ailing girl under the tent helped me to justify the girl's predicament. God punished wickedness, convent school piety had taught me. If people suffered, it must be their fault. This at least was logical.

As a result, whenever my body malfunctioned, I began to feel obscurely guilty, and even today I associate depression with sin. Perhaps this was why my several violent attacks of appendicitis during the previous winter in boarding school had been kept a secret from my mother, by me as well as by the nuns. Of what had my sinfulness consisted? Hypocrisy, no doubt. To pretend to be healthy must be just as false as to pretend to be good. I had even hidden my dislike of convent school behind a front of exaggerated cheerfulness.

* * *

Mother had decided that I must be exposed to the best cultural opportunities, the refinements of the Parisian language, and all the advantages the great city had to offer. No doubt she longed to live there, to remove herself as well as me from the tensions developing in our household, but my only desire was to stay at home, to explore my own territory, to observe the mysteries going on behind garden walls. All that summer Sylvia and I climbed onto our wall to check on the monsignor's niece. At night, lying in bed in the room we shared, we wondered what evil deed she could have done to deserve this long wasting away of her body.

Then, in September, I left for Paris and forgot all about the girl in the tent. I had been prepared for life in the great capital with a book full of somber photographs: the bearded Verlaine and young Rimbaud drinking absinthe in a café called Hell, Sarah Bernhardt sleeping in her coffin, and the gnome Toulouse-Lautrec peering through his monocle at the music hall singer La Goulue.

In my mind Aunt Jeanne, with whom I would be staying, was one of these doomed characters. But to my surprise, she glowed with a physical warmth to which I was not accustomed. Mother was rather reserved, evasive. Jeanne immediately clasped Mother and me to her bosom, at the same time bursting out laughing.

"What in heaven's name are you wearing?" she exclaimed, twirling Mother around. It was the white fur coat. "You look like a sheep. And the poor little one? You'd think she were an orphan." My mother had thought that a red belt would be enough to disguise my black convent uniform, which was made of such indestructible material that it would be a shame not to wear it out. That night, as I fell asleep, I heard the two sisters talking, talking, and much later, when I woke briefly, they were still at it, lying together in Jeanne's bed in the dark. "Don't be a sheep, *voyons*," Jeanne was saying, and the next day when Mother left for home she was wearing Jeanne's leopardskin, in which she looked much less vulnerable.

Jeanne lived in an old building with creaking parquet floors. There was no man in the apartment, which did not seem right. In the convent there had been God, who smelt of incense, but Jeanne's apartment smelled strongly of Chanel perfume. She spent most evenings, when she thought I was asleep, calling her former husband, René Moulaert, who was a stage designer. I could understand her bitter reproaches. He owed her money; he lived with an actress. Yet was it not her fault, since she had run off with Wiegersma? Her misfortunes, too, must be the punishment for sin. Once she spoke to me as if I were an adult of the man in Holland who, she said, had ruined her life. She pronounced his name, which I had heard mentioned only with hatred, fear, and ridicule, with the deep throaty tones of love.

"I shall never regret it," she said. "He was larger than life. His energy overwhelmed me." I longed to hear more, spellbound by her love, which also seemed larger than life, but she now hid her melancholy behind the smokescreen of her cigarette, which she inhaled deeply, lifting her eyes to the ceiling. Her depression was contagious. Then, as if touched by my emergence from childhood, she smiled at me with melancholy tenderness, calling me *ma cocotte*, and I longed to kiss her fleshy cheeks and warm brown skin. Her hips in tight skirts were voluptuous. I loved to catch her by surprise and encircle them with my arms, which made her stumble and laugh.

Now her most constant visitor was a youngish man, half paralyzed with polio, whom she doted on like a son. She called him *mon coco* and told him he looked like a painting by El Greco, but he dragged his left leg, and his left hand was convulsed into an ugly claw. He had dark, burning eyes and one side of his face was stiff and immobile. He took a liking to me and engaged me in conversations, stuttering painfully, but terrified of his ugliness I blushed with embarrassment in his presence. He began to meet me, as if by chance, as I walked home from school through the Luxembourg Gardens. In my dreams he became a huge spider standing between me and the sunlight, weaving a web about me that I could not escape. Ashamed of being associated with him, I hurried home through the park, hoping to avoid him as well as the exhibitionists who pursued me wherever I went.

I realized of course that I was being uncharitable, and on Sundays, to atone for this sin, went to Mass at Saint Sulpice. Then I visited the Louvre to look at the *Mona Lisa,* for art, too, was a religion in which I worshiped. Aunt Jeanne, exhausted after working in an office all week, stayed in bed eating chocolates, and having fulfilled my duties I rushed home to creep under her silk eiderdown with her, whiffing the perfume on her neck.

One afternoon I was alone in the apartment when the doorbell rang. There, armed with an umbrella and a suitcase, respectably hatted and wearing her characteristic expression of determination, stood my indomitable Bonne Maman, recently returned from Mexico. She had embarked on this journey at the age of sixty-five, trekked into wild mountainous territory with an Indian guide on muleback. She had broken a leg, gotten robbed twice, been poisoned by a snakebite, and become an expert on Aztec civilization. Now she had come to Paris because there was to be a lecture on the Aztecs at the natural history museum.

With the intention of exposing me to all cultural advantages, she took me along. It was a documentary film on the customs of certain Mexican tribes, and all I remember is one endless close-up of a woman in childbirth. Dressed in a white linen gown, she stood on the porch of a cabin, her arms tied to the ceiling so she would not be tempted to sit down. Suspended by her wrist, she moaned and twisted endlessly until finally her husband took a rope, tied it around her waist and began to pull while she screamed with pain. My grandmother found this fascinating.

The next morning we set off on foot, Bonne Maman in the lead, I following with the umbrella. She recited names and dates while we marched along the quays, gray stone parapets, and towers of the Conciergerie and through echoing halls burdened with history and the tombs of the great. I decided deep within my stubborn head that I did not love Paris, would not remember anything, and had only one desire—to go home to the provinces. At the bird market, yellow canaries fluttered in their cages like imprisoned sunlight.

The climax to this endless day was hot chocolate and croissants in a *patisserie* on the Boulevard Saint-Michel, but the thick syrup with whipped cream made me very ill. "Are your eyes bigger than your stomach?" asked Bonne Maman with a knowing smile. Her eyes were concerned as she nodded at me in her deaf way, and suddenly she too inspired me with guilt for not loving her the way one ought to love a grandmother.

She returned to St. Truiden and I lay in the apartment retching for days, watched over with fatalistic indifference by Aunt Jeanne's maid, who wore embroidered slippers and smelled of cheap perfume. An ex–music-hall singer with frizzy red hair and painted lips, she kept singing, "Spring is about to be born and I am about to die." Since spring was approaching distantly, the implication seemed clear, though the song was really about Marie Antoinette waiting for her execution. Finally, one Sunday afternoon while the crippled young man was having tea with Aunt Jeanne, I lay, flushed with fever, listening to his halting, stuttering voice. Nausea welled up and I rushed through the living room to the cold bathroom where I stood in bare feet on the brick floor, vomiting, remembering the twisted face of the unfortunate creature whose presence seemed somehow responsible in my mind for my illness. That night I was rushed to the hospital and operated on in the nick of time for appendicitis.

The crippled man visited me in the hospital, attentive, bringing flowers, but his presence seemed to imply that now I would become crooked like him. It was not until my mother came and kept watch by my bed that I felt safe. She brought me a large pear to eat and read me Father's daily letters. He described his own symptoms, caused by the worry I had occasioned him, and his retreat to his bed, where he had lain sympathizing for two whole days. I laughed at this until my stitches hurt, imagining him wallowing in his stained-glass bed, his head wrapped in a knitted scarf to protect him from drafts. I begged Mother to take me home. "Won't you miss Aunt Jeanne?" she asked me.

"This is no place for a child, *voyons*," said Jeanne, scolding Mother with sibling authority.

And so we returned together to the house in Roermond, where childhood might be prolonged a little longer.

And the monsignor's niece? I had forgotten her until Father decided I should be tutored in Latin, a passion of his that he wanted to share with me but that the local school I now attended considered unnecessary for females. In order that I might continue my study of it, he called Monsignor Thyssen, who, he now revealed, had been his own Latin professor at the boys' seminary he used to attend.

One afternoon, overcome with shyness, I rang the door-bell of the monsignor's house around the corner. He opened the door himself, welcomed me warmly, and led me up the steep stairs to his study, a pleasant room with leather armchairs, Persian rugs, and the smell of good cigars. The double window veiled by lace curtains opened onto the garden, and suddenly the memory of the tent and the dying girl obsessed me. Was she still there? Had she survived the long winter? The monsignor, with brusque friendliness, tried to put me at ease, telling stories about my father's school pranks, and how he had invented a game on the playground, throwing discus with the wooden lids from the outhouses. But the Latin lesson became an uncomfortable blur as I tried to summon the courage to ask him what illness had done to his niece while I had been struggling with mine. I must have shown a remarkable lack of aptitude. Puzzled, the man looked at me with concern and jumped up to summon his housekeeper to prepare tea for me.

The minute he left the room, I ran to the window and, pushing the curtain aside, saw that the pavilion was gone.

9
THE WALLET

In the summer of 1939 we began to run away again, as we had so many years before. Repeatedly we packed ourselves into the car with bags of flour, sugar, and sausages and took to the road. This time it was not Henk Wiegersma that threatened us, but the invasion of Austria, disturbing border incidents, and a general mobilization.

We practiced wearing our gas masks, looking like insects with huge eyes and proboscises. The vaulted stone cellar under the house where the wine was kept became a bomb shelter. In the kitchen the maids described the atrocities the Germans had committed in Belgium during the first world war: cutting off children's hands, raping women, and setting villages on fire.

Mother began to hoard old clothes that were especially warm and sturdy in case fuel should get scarce. She seemed less hysterical than other people about taking precautions, and appeared instead to be simply preparing for an exciting journey. The difference was that, as a Belgian, she was an experienced refugee. She had fled, as a child, with her mother and sisters to England and then Scotland, France, and Italy, and had enjoyed it tremendously. In fact, Italy had been Mother's America, a place where one escaped the monotony of ordinary life, a place of adventure and romance. Now that it was a fascist country, however, it would no longer do.

I used to wonder why we fled. None of the neighbors did. They laughed and teased us. "There isn't going to be a war!" they said. Was it simply a habit of restlessness with Mother, or did she feel the need to get away from Ficelle? Later, when I learned about racial persecutions, I wondered if we were perhaps Jews. Was it for our sake, the safety of the children? Was my father a coward? Was it his horror of fascism that uprooted us? Or was it merely a practical consideration that drove us away, the fact that stained glass was so purely a peacetime commodity?

We first drove south and stayed with friends near Brussels. There had never been so much fruit as there was that year. "Just as in 1914, it's a sign!" people said. The meadows and the wheat fields were full of poppies, cornflowers, and daisies — red, white, and blue, the colors of the Dutch flag. I longed to pick them all before the Germans came, as if they were treasures not to be left behind. After a few days, the storm of fear blew over and Father relaxed. Our exile turned into a pleasant holiday and I gorged on *gaufrettes,* delicious wafers made by our hostess's cook, and on the tender greens grown in the vegetable garden.

Another time we fled north along roads clogged with army transports full of soldiers dressed in green, young boys herded together in trucks, waiting, like us, for something to happen, for traffic to resume its normal course. They waved at us and smiled.

"Why should we not return to our house by the sea?" I asked. I was quite certain no Germans would find us there, and we would be as safe as in an egg, the egg out of which I had hatched. Groet remained my Eden, though in the last few years we had not gone there. "It's too far away from schools," said my mother, "and too difficult to heat." But in my heart I accused her of unfaithfulness, of not loving that house as it deserved to be loved. Instead, she rented a horrid suburban cottage, with varnished paneling on the walls, in a town called Bergen, presumably behind the defense lines, enrolled us in a progressive school, and left us there with Anna while she herself returned to Roermond, where, in the old family house, a world was being dismantled. Father, having been offered a job painting murals in New York, had hurriedly sold the house as well as the glass studio to his business manager, who had unexpectedly come up with an offer. This man was a German, and the thought of his pudgy daughter sleeping in our bed, eating at the pink, mirrored glass table seemed outrageous, as if the enemy had already taken over.

When she heard all this, Anna wept and hid her bloodless face behind her limp blond hair, which she had just washed in the kitchen sink. Usually coiled in a tight braid, it now shrouded her in tiny wavelets, like the hair of a Mary Magdalen.

"What is the matter?" I asked, having only recently become aware that Anna was not just a servant but a touching, devoted human being.

"You are going to America and you will forget all about me," she sniffed and began to sew traveling outfits for our dolls, two identical wooden heads with cloth bodies, both called Bijou, which Mother had made for us. Though we had outgrown them, we carried them along everywhere as talismans. Anna took us on a bicycle trip for a last look at our house by the sea, of which she was as fond as we. It was a gray autumn day and we struggled upwind along the empty polders, my sister on Anna's bicycle rack, clinging to her waist. There it stood, modestly squatting under its hat of thatch behind the rose hip hedge, the face of happiness.

But the house was rented to a horrid woman who must have thought we had come to collect the rent, for she slammed the door in our faces and we turned back with tears in our eyes.

Only once more did we return to Roermond. There was a strange, febrile coming and going in the house and we were everywhere in the way. Objects were being sold, and others crated. In the dining room stood dust-covered rows of bottles of ancient wine, the entire contents of the wine cellar, accumulated through the years by Bompa and Father, which now had to be drunk up in a month. In the midst of this feverish atmosphere of departure, corks were continually popping, glasses were lifted against the light to show the ruby colors Father had tried to reproduce in his windows, and the mellow velvety wine was rolled upon the tongue in an exquisite ecstasy.

Like the drinking, everything was now done in a hurry. I parted from school friends; from my gilt-edged, red-bound books with engraved illustrations; from the garden into which one could lean from the bedroom windows; from the circular creaking stairs, the black and white stone pavement in the hall, the four steps down the front stoop, and the narrow, brick-paved street.

Ficelle put Sylvia and me on the train to Bergen. "They are going to America," she told the soldiers in the compartment, as if this meant we were precious and would they please take care of us. They were impressed and asked us if we were not afraid of mines. "What are mines?" I inquired. And they, were they not afraid of fighting the Germans? With the peculiar "tell-me-another-one" humorous expression of the Dutch, they shrugged their shoulders and smiled. "There's not going to be a war," they said.

We wore new matching beige coats with fur-trimmed hoods, and I felt important and dazed as the train crept slowly north with its load of singing soldiers, across the great bridges over the Maas and the Waal that were to be

blown up should the Germans attack. Then came the flat
polders and the dikes, which could be broken to flood the
land and stop the advancing enemy.

"In the north we are safe," the soldiers said. "Don't you
know your history? We've done it before." I saw the protective water glistening in the night. With my cheek against
the cold pane, I peered out the window at this country I
loved and would be leaving for fifteen years.

We were to sail in December, a few days before
Christmas. When Father joined us he was quite lopsided,
and kept fingering and patting a huge wallet in his breast
pocket. It contained our identities, our passage to a new
life, and our entire fortune. I was very impressed by this
and by the renewed importance vested in my father, its
carrier, whom I was determined to keep in sight at all times.
With much nervous giggling, Mother and Ficelle hid the
wallet overnight, but the next day we left for Rotterdam
from where we were to sail, the precious packet once more
reinstated in the breast pocket.

At the U.S. embassy, we stood in line for hours, and
Father, twitching all over with impatience and nervous
tension, kept running to the front of the line, pulling out
the wallet to bribe officials, saying in a loud voice, "I am
Joep Nicolas," much to our embarrassment and with no
success at all. The slow, anonymous processes of democracy
were at work. We were told to undress, and together with a
lot of strangers, were given physical examinations, as if we
were cattle.

Ficelle decided we must have elegant dresses in New
York. Until then, we had always been dressed by seam-
stresses or by Anna, who knitted sweaters and embroidered
with flowers or white pigeons summer dresses designed by
Mother. This time we went to a big department store in
Rotterdam and were outfitted in black patent leather
pumps, white socks, and pale blue, pleated Liberty dresses
with round collars and belts. Everyone blinked when they

saw me in mine, for it was a little girl's outfit and I looked preposterous, but this was apparently the wrong moment to insist that I was no longer a child. In the evening, an orchid was pinned to my awkward bosom. Crowds of people came to say good-bye at a farewell dinner. There were press photographers, Father talked on the radio, and I heard someone say bitterly, "The rats are leaving the sinking ship." Ladies I hardly knew sobbed and I was kissed by a strange gentleman called, I was told, "Simon the Magician." Hovering forlorn in the background stood Anna, clutching a huge red pocketbook we had given her as a farewell present, the only reward for ten years of devotion. Then suddenly we were at the other end of the gangplank looking down at Ficelle doing a comic dance, throwing kisses, appearing and disappearing as in an absurd puppet show.

We were completely alone, the four of us, in our first-class cabins as the ship sailed off hooting into the night, and I wondered how we had gotten there, whose idea it had been, and whether it was a good thing. Suddenly, we all seemed very vulnerable: Father with his enormous wallet, balding at the temples, smiling at us distantly as if he didn't see us at all; Mother with circles under her eyes and her orchids pinned askew; Sylvia innocently delighted with the upper bunk; and I weighed down by my tremendous feeling of responsibility, as if I were the grandmother of us all.

We lived in luxury, courtesy of the Holland America Line. Caviar was wheeled to our table in windmills made of ice. But as I walked around the deck, keeping a close watch on Father and his wallet, I could not help looking down once in a while at the third-class deck where refugees huddled in seasick clusters. "They are Jews," Father explained. I believe I had never heard the word before. Since we were all in the same boat, I decided we were all fleeing the same danger for the same reason.

Danger, danger – it was everywhere around us on that voyage, in the waves hiding mines, in the wind bringing wild storms and tossing the ship. Naively I took comfort in the fact that I was a good swimmer. Yet it was in the seemingly safe red velvet parlor, where the many mirrors were framed in gold, where an orchestra played in the evening, that danger lurked. My parents had made friends with anyone not too seasick to appear on deck: an entire ballet company, a scholarly gentleman, a lonely young lady, and a sinister Russian couple.

These last were very knowing about what to expect in America and began giving Father advice. The lady, a fading beauty with plucked eyebrows, smiled at me condescendingly and told me I had "good legs," which I knew to be flattery. Distrustful, I began to think of this pair as the fox and the wolf who convinced Pinocchio to plant his money in the field of gold. Repeatedly I found them huddled together with Father over one of the little tables, suddenly interrupting their conversation because of the presence of "children." Finally, on the last day of the voyage, the burden of the wallet proved to be too much for Father and he signed half his capital over to the Russians to be invested in a company in Canada. This company went bankrupt immediately and we never saw the Russians again, but when Father appeared on deck the next morning he looked greatly relieved and much more symmetrical. "I don't have money but I make it," I had always heard him boast. Artists relied on their gifts and wits rather than on a fortune. Disembarking in the capital of capitalism, he would face it on his own terms.

Then it rose out of the sea, the strange country of gangsters, Indians, kidnappers, and endless possibilities. But when we saw the low, snowy coastline of Long Island, Mother's face fell. "It looks just like Holland," she said. "I'd hoped for something more exotic, more like Italy." The Statue of Liberty and lower Manhattan, grimly black against the snow and gray sky, were awesome enough, but the docks at Hoboken could not have been more dismal. "Go comb your hair," Father told his female chorus, by now used to attracting attention wherever we went. "The press will be aboard any minute." Meekly we obeyed, but though we were almost the last passengers to walk down the gangplank in the icy wind to wait by the letter N for our luggage, not a soul had come to meet us, much less take our photographs. We had landed alone and unknown in a new world.

10
IN SEARCH
OF PRÉ

"Mottom Sholder," it says. "Rosted chikken. Pré soop sur-
ved with raspt chees." These recipes are written in a neat
round hand in a notebook with yellowed paper I found
among abandoned bric-a-brac when my parents returned
to Europe.

"Omelette. Put butter, little onions, choped pré and par-
selie in a friing pan. Let it brown. Poor the eggs. Stur till
they take consistance. When it take collar turn it."

Immediately I recognized the spelling as my mother's
creative amalgam of all the languages she spoke in her life,
for this is the cookbook of a wanderer, a bird of many nests,
a refugee by predilection. The cookbook was very much a
part of the nest she built for us in New York, in a duplex
studio apartment on West Sixty-seventh Street. The best of
our Dutch furniture had been brought over, including
some enormous baroque cabinets, which were much too
large for New York apartments and which began to crack in
the central heating, as well as the awkward stained-glass

bed. Father's paintings hung on the wall. China bibelots bought in a junk shop in Alkmaar, African sculpture Uncle Charles had brought back from the Gold Coast, Delft vases, Bonne Maman's Victorian doll—all this was supposed to make us feel at home. Yet these transplanted objects talked only of the past. They dragged us down with the weight of their nostalgia. And so at first we were utterly bewildered, all of us, even Mother, who had thought this move would be just another adventure, like her wanderings during the first war.

When she talked about those years of her childhood, her round, childish eyes had a dreamy look. With her incredible memory for vivid details, she took us along with her to the London boardinghouse for Belgian refugees where the red-headed cook sheltered a monkey between her breasts; to the country house where the butler served pineapples grown in the hothouse and where she spent Christmas trying to teach French to her stone-deaf hostess; to Glasgow, where she read all of Dickens and went to embroidery school; to the lakes of Scotland, where she and her sisters went on walking tours in the rain; to Paris, where they starved; and to Forte dei Marmi, where she had fourteen boyfriends.

"But how about the war?" I asked.

"Oh, yes, there was a war. We had very little food and we got chilblains from the cold." But who needs food when one has fourteen boyfriends? And who needs spelling, really, so long as one can converse with people? And so Mother went to art school and developed a passion for sculpture.

But in New York, communication could be difficult. For one thing, our maids were an odd assortment of refugees from all over the world, and even if they could read English, Mother's recipes could only puzzle them. "What is this *pré*?" they asked. "I never heard of *pré*."

"But without *pré* nothing tastes the same!" Mother frowned and went in search of it in the supermarkets and the Italian greengrocers on Columbus Avenue.

"What?" they shrugged. "How do you spell it?"

"Perhaps it's spelled *p-r-a-y*. Or could it be *p-r-e-y?*"

It was no use. Our first maid, a blowsy Cockney, wife to a policeman, was handed the notebook and told to manage without *pré*. The book read:

Monday: Mottom sholder. Butter brown in pan. Add the sholder. Let it take collar. Cover with water. Add celeri, pré, onion, turnip, carottes, pepper. Cook few hours.

Tuesday: Oxtail soop. Cotelettes of veel with herbs. Pré au gratin. Baked potatoos and appel sauce.

Wednesday: Rosted duck. Put the duck if he is to fat without butter in the oven. In a pan put butter. Ad the duck of which fat is melted away with an onion, time, one half lorrel leave. Stur the liquid with a littel flower. Ad a glass of red wine or lemon juce. You may fill him with choped meet.

The English cook sighed, confused. But since she made a good roast beef with Yorkshire pudding, we did not fare badly at all, though it got monotonous. Alas, she did not stay long. After her came a lovely Austrian lady who was so elegant and attractive that all the gentlemen who visited us fell in love with her. Unfortunately she could only make cakes, such rich and beautiful cakes, filled with ground nuts and butter cream, that we all got indigestion eating them. They were very expensive and took a great deal of time to prepare and their cook attracted too many admirers. She soon went on to better things and Mother found a Jewish refugee from Germany, a young girl only a few years older than myself who was lonely and unhappy and, besides, much too intellectual for cooking. We felt very sorry for her, and she for herself, so that we all cleaned and cooked rather than see her dissolve into tears. She, too, moved on, to our great relief.

Then came a tiny, desiccated Puerto Rican woman, a fiery creature who spoke only Spanish and who cleaned with passion. I was sick with a high fever that winter, and while she was mopping the floor in my room, I was taken with a violent nosebleed. I begged her for ice or a cold water compress but she stared at me with her dull black eyes and shook her head uncomprehendingly. Watching the blood pouring out of my nose, she got the idea that I was dying, fell on her knees, and began to shout an endless litany that I recognized as the prayers for the dead.

After that, the Puerto Rican developed a frightening wheeze and became too sick to come to work. She was replaced by a Hungarian who made goulash and strudel. We watched her stretching sheets of strudel dough all over the kitchen. She rolled it and pulled it and hung it on the backs of chairs and towel racks. A calm, majestic black woman replaced her, and she too with hope was handed the recipe notebook.

Thursday: Pee soop. Put in the water bones, potatoos, two onions, one salad, pré, pees with their shelfes. Sift with little breads frijed.

The black lady nodded and smiled and cooked us a Southern fry. Since Mother's susceptible stomach suffered from the fat in this otherwise delectable dish, she began to cook for us herself while the maid kept under control the fine soot that settled on every surface now that it was spring and the windows wide open. From then on we ate delicate and delicious meals: kidnees, brest of veel, spinedge through the sift, letuce stoved, choped meat in a kake. I myself, out of nostalgia for my Dutch grandmother, undertook the cooking of vlan, or custard pudding. Though Mother was amazed at my proficiency at making vlan, her activities were so numerous by now and she had become so high-strung that she was unable to digest anything but tea and boiled rice.

That first summer, she decided the city would be unhealthy for us and took a job as an art counselor in a camp on a lake smothered by trees. We performed in its production of *Orpheus,* in which she appeared as Venus, a shimmering vision of beauty, but I could tell that the virgin forest depressed her, for she repeatedly mentioned the Tuscan landscape, with its cultivated fields, its oxen and rows of grapevines. When we returned to New York she hired a studio in a basement down the street where she gave sculpture lessons to society ladies and started a button factory. There was a wartime restriction on metal buttons at that time and her plaster ones were a great success. Her assistant was Jacques Schiffrin, a French gentleman with a long nose who had been a publisher of luxury editions in Paris. Now he was pouring plaster, cleaning molds, and painting buttons while she dashed off to Saks and Bergdorf Goodman's to take orders. She also made plaster frames for gift shops and *putti* carved in wood.

She did interior decorating jobs, made statues for nightclubs, taught in a school in Westchester County, made portraits of celebrities, and had a successful sculpture exhibition. All this with a modest, matter-of-fact air, for she was the kind of small woman who kept in the background and let her husband do the talking. When someone noticed her, she was always surprised.

"Strange, why do you suppose so-and-so likes me?" she would ask. Then, flattered, she would accept dinner invitations from gentlemen. Without warning them, she would bring her daughters along, which was not at all what they had in mind. In fact, we became a threesome for better or worse, and sometimes I was jealous of her. When I began to have beaus, they preferred to stay home and talk to her and eat her meals rather than take me out to the movies. On

summer evenings, we walked in Central Park and the
sailors whistled at her and tried to pick her up.

After dinner, when we had done the dishes, she put on
her hat and coat and went back to her studio. "I'll just wet
my statue," she'd say. Then, at three in the morning, Father
would burst into our bedrooms in great alarm. "Where is
your mother? Did she run away?" He seemed to consider it
a constant danger that she would abandon us and simply
disappear. I, too, always imagined some terrible disaster
and, pulling on my clothes, would rush out in the night to
that basement studio. There she would stand, her hat and
coat still on, her pocketbook hanging on her arm, absorbed
in touching up a clay figure, called *Liberation*, of a woman
caught in a cagelike structure with arms and legs reaching
out through the bars. That familiar routine of hers, stepping back, looking sideways, adding some clay here, wiping
some away there . . . she went on doing it as if there were
nothing unusual in my finding her like this, the night
watchman coming after me to check up on the situation.

It was to this studio that I would run for consolation and
sympathy, but she was such a strange mixture of old-
fashioned, earthy wisdom and progressive experimental-
ism that her advice could be baffling. If I were shrinking
from difficulties at school, wanting to stay in bed and hide,
she would lend me her best suit and silk stockings and send
me off to face my problems boldly. If I felt guilty at some
mischief we had done and came and confessed to her, she
would burst out laughing. When a homosexual asked me to
marry him, she cocked her head pensively, shrugged her
shoulders, and said, "Why not try it for a while?"

Sometimes, prey to some nameless melancholy, I would
make a scene, scream and cry, and she would calmly watch,
calling my sister in to share the spectacle. They would both
sit there and giggle while I carried on. Thus I learned to
control myself and not to count on their sympathy. Later,
when we were at a party and I, all dressed up, was talking

with self-assurance to someone, I caught her staring at me as if astonished that I could communicate with strangers and was no longer in need of her protection. "I think you'll become a strong woman, just like me," she said.

But most surprising were her religious scruples. She'd challenge me with the remark, "You and I, we are too rational to believe in God." Yet the next moment would reveal her superstitions. She was, at the time, competing for a big commission, a statue of *Christ, Light of the World,* and was chosen as one of the three finalists. To win the commission became her great hope. She waited in suspense, but finally lost. She then told me the real reason for this failure. "You passed your examinations because you went to Mass first, whereas I promised God that I would go to Mass every Sunday until He gave me the prize. Well, you know, I never kept my promise, so of course He in turn forgot about me."

Poor Mother! Why should this kind of bargaining with God matter to her suddenly? She got discouraged and talked quite often about Fate and Luck. "Do you know that the destiny line in your father's hand is disappearing?" she asked me, and when things took a brief turn for the better she'd whisper to me excitedly, "How long do you think my luck will last?"

In 1942, when the whole country was plunged into the war effort, she decided she must do her bit and began to take a night course in Brooklyn to learn how to make precision instruments. She'd come home on the subway in the middle of the night, and it was then that her health finally broke down. For weeks she lay in the dark bedroom in the glass bed, mending our socks. Then she began to consult doctors with strange cures and theories, taking me along, since I was very underweight. I was put on an insulin cure and after each shot would arrive home fainting with hunger. One of her doctors told me that my appendix had grown back and would have to be removed again, that he had removed his own wife's appendix three times. From then on, I refused to go to a doctor ever again. But Mother had operations, bought an orthopedic corset for her backache, and went to an osteopath. I felt obscurely that the reason for her illnesses was some unhappiness she could not diagnose, loneliness possibly, but being caught in the selfishness of adolescence, I was of little comfort to her.

She had a few eccentric friends who drank, had nervous breakdowns, and went on diets, and who gave her their old hats like bird's nests, slightly faded and flattened out as if someone had sat on them. An old gentleman offered her his moth-eaten raccoon coat. She was photographed for *Town and Country* in a flattering white suit, but it had been borrowed.

How different it all was from the nomad's existence during World War I! As in her recipes, some subtle element seemed to be missing, elusive as that word *pré*, of which she had forgotten the English and had never learned the spelling.

It is only now, when I read her cookbook again, that it suddenly dawns on me what she was looking for: in Dutch, *prij*, in French *poireau*, in Italian *porro*, meaning "leek" — a noble vegetable that gives body and flavor to dishes but was hard to find in this country in those days, especially if one asked for *pré*.

II
THE CAGE

In those days Father lived in a cage. He paced up and down, back and forth, like the wolf in the Central Park Zoo, and the swirls of smoke from his cigar rose up to where I stood watching him behind a pillar of the balcony that looked down into the pit of his two-story studio.

In the riding stable across the street, horses were being shod and the clanking of iron was reminiscent of the blacksmith in Groet. Horses' hooves rang out on the pavement as riders went back and forth to the park, and horses looked out of the third-floor windows across from my room. Through the long afternoon the voices of singers doing their scales rose and fell, climbed ladders by threes, missed the highest, broke off and started again, over and over, for several voice teachers lived in our building. Like those singers endlessly pursuing that high note, Father was pursuing something elusive and difficult through the chimeras of his cigar smoke. I wondered what it was exactly as I watched him fight off the interruptions, the endless intrusions of a troubled world.

One night in spring I woke up to the sound of him talking excitedly in Dutch over the telephone. It worried me, but I fell asleep again and decided the next morning that I had had a bad dream.

Sylvia was already in the kitchen frying herself an egg. She led a life quite independent of mine. Although we both went to the French *lycée,* we took separate buses uptown, she along Madison Avenue and I on Eighth, where I met a Belgian friend called Kiki.

As soon as I stepped on the bus I was surrounded by a wall of newspapers with headlines reading "HOLLAND AND BELGIUM INVADED." As I looked at those letters they began to dance uncontrollably in front of my eyes, and when Kiki joined me at Eighty-sixth Street we fell into each other's arms and began to cry. "And I wasn't even there," I sobbed, remembering the task Mr. Pimput had prescribed for me. But this time surely my attention would have been useless. We were lucky to be safe in America, reading all those impersonal headlines.

We felt alone on that bus, orphans without a country. We walked across the park, which had just burst into bloom, crazily green, and the tenderness of spring was an added affront to the sadness of this day. In school the other students surrounded us with deferential silence, as if there had been deaths in our families. "They're resisting bravely, I hear, the Dutch," said someone, but bravery had nothing to do with it, I felt. It was somehow intensely humiliating, this invasion of our countries, and both of us dreaded going home. Instead we sat under a cherry tree and talked about cherries, gardens, boating on rivers, and drinking grenadine that had been kept cool in a cellar, and about swimming in pools, brooks, muddy rivers, the North Sea. We bought popsicles and lay in the grass, dreaming about summer dresses, then walked slowly first to her house, then to mine, then back to hers again.

When I finally went home no one noticed me. For five days Father had ears only for the news and remained glued to a little radio he had bought for the occasion. I thought that if only he would turn the radio off the news would miraculously get better, but he didn't give it a chance and remained huddled in a corner, leaning toward the apocalyptic voice. I began to consider the invasion of our country as an invasion of his person, as if his passive body were being trampled by armies, parachutists dropping behind the facade of his face and the troubled geography of his brow.

From then on I fled from home as much as possible and accompanied Kiki to roller-skating rinks and to Woolworth's, where we bought transparent Tangee lipstick and a cactus in a miniature Chinese pagoda.

Sylvia too, though only twelve, had a mysterious private life. She disappeared for entire afternoons and brought home Gershwin records or books about oddly adult subjects such as Savonarola or Casanova.

"Where do you get the money?" I asked her, for my expenditures were much more modest.

"I empty Father's pockets at night. He hates small change," she explained candidly. Then, during rare evenings when our parents went out, we dressed up in their clothes and danced to the music. I was beginning to depend on Sylvia to entertain me. Every evening I looked forward to her return from downtown, which she explored on her own, and caught her as she tiptoed up the stairs so as not to disturb Father at work.

"Where have you been?" I whispered. If she answered "None of your business," we'd fight, Father would shout at us to be quiet, and we'd slam doors. Once she came into my room and performed an entire Marx Brothers movie she had seen at the Museum of Modern Art. She was especially good at Harpo and made me laugh till the tears ran down my cheeks. Another time she'd been to the Natural History Museum, where a dark man in a cape had followed her from dinosaurs to whales, until she managed to escape and ran all the way home. Her adventures were much more daring than my childish afternoons with Kiki.

The following school year, a new influx of students arrived at the *lycée*, refugees from occupied France. Among them were aristocrats with such names as Bourbon and Uzès de Crussol, but also sons and daughters of actors and artists, Sorbonne professors, and even, it was whispered in the halls, the great-grandson of Victor Hugo. This created an excitement that made school a heady place to be. The newcomers spoke Parisian slang and were noisy and slightly insolent, the way only the French, who consider themselves the most sophisticated people in the world, can be.

"Have you seen the one they call the movie star?" asked Kiki. I was beginning to find her excessive devotion to me annoying. When we took the bus together, she would kick me in the shins and murmur through closed lips with an insinuating grin, "That man is staring at you." I had recently been persuaded to stop wearing my glasses, for I was practicing something called the Bates System, which consisted largely of guessing at what I saw rather than seeing it. Still, I felt beautiful for the first time in my life even though I missed out on men staring at me, and refused to believe Kiki who, I was convinced, had *l'esprit mal tourné*, a one-track mind.

One day she hoisted herself onto the bus pink-cheeked and eager to impart some momentous news. "Guess what," she exclaimed. "The movie star has fallen in love with you." She was so excited by this that she had forgotten to button her jumper in the back and her plump bare thighs were quite naked. I blushed with embarrassment at her appearance as well as her announcement. Obviously, this talk of love was foolishness.

I was only vaguely aware of the boy in question. He had copper-colored hair and blue eyes and played soccer energetically in the courtyard, kicking the ball into the steel gate so that the dull thud echoed between the walls. In English class he sat in the back row and seemed bored, his long legs stretched out under the desk, which was too small for him. Though it was midwinter, his skin had a brown glow. He obviously shaved, for he did not have the tender down on his upper lip that many of my classmates still had. His hands were unusually wide and muscular, his voice deep and full. His indifference to the rest of us seemed rather conceited, and when asked a question he refused at first to answer in English, feigning complete ignorance.

"He gives himself airs," I had told Kiki.

"He needs a haircut. Do you think he bleaches it?"

"He has cruel hands and a Spanish name. Spaniards are cruel and conceited."

But today Kiki was obviously under his spell.

"I promise you, it's true," she said. "He stopped me in the hall yesterday after school and asked me lots of personal questions about you. He told me he hadn't slept all night and had drunk all of his mother's vermouth."

"A whole bottle? Are you sure? He must have been bragging." When we got off at Ninety-sixth Street, three boys met behind us, shook hands energetically, then followed us.

"It's him," hissed Kiki. Suddenly I knew I was being watched, observed. It was a loss of freedom.

In English class this arrogant "movie star" made a beeline for the desk next to mine and threw down his books with a proprietary air. "It's mine," he announced loudly, defying Kiki and a mortician's son with a bobbing Adam's apple, who had become attentive after I took off my glasses.

I was a good English student. "Black is the night that covers me . . . ," I recited with properly stoic gloom. But perhaps because the mood of the world was so black that winter, ours was one of irreverent levity. Struck by the jingle and bounce of English anapests, I had written a pastiche that began

> I'd like to see angels sometimes in the sky
> On broad flapping wings as they gently float by . . .

This had been published in the school paper and from then on I was considered gifted, even though I had meant it as a joke.

"Kiki says you write poems," the young man next to me now ventured. His smile was dazzling, overwhelming, and I felt invaded by it. His hand on the desk, so close to mine, was disturbing. He talked loudly, so that everyone could hear, and the teacher, annoyed, tried to call him to order by asking him to recite Keats's "Ode to Autumn." "Season of mists and mellow fruitfulness. . . ." Whether it was the resonance of his voice, his surprisingly good accent, or his sensitivity to Keats, the poem rang in my ears like music, the English language muscular and precise.

The teacher, impressed, gave him a nineteen on twenty. The young man, called Jean Alvarez de Toledo, acknowledged this compliment with an ingratiating bow of the head, then continued his conversation with me as if the classroom did not exist.

"I hear you are from Holland." Then, with a taunting smile, "My ancestors were the Inquisitors of your country at one time."

"They were monsters," I said fiercely.

"Yes," he agreed, and smiled as if this were a charming trait, sure to endear him to me. The whole class was watching us. The teacher's voice rose angrily at the blackboard.

"This is an English class, if you please!"

To which Jean answered politely, "All right. We'll talk in English. Your father is a painter of stained glass," he continued. "I am a great admirer of Chartres Cathedral."

"He is Modern," I said defensively. "Not Medieval."

"My father is a seducer of women," reported Jean. "He climbs into girls' windows at night."

"How horrible!"

"Yes. He was at one time ambassador to the Vatican and abandoned me in a small village in Italy, where I lived with the priest. Neither of us had any shoes." Exotic, I thought. He is trying to charm me with the oddities of his life.

"Then why did you flee Europe? Spain is not at war. It is an ally to the Nazis."

"My father is a refugee from the Spanish Civil War." This meant his father was a hero in the cause of antifascism. It made him more glamorous than my father, who painted on glass. Reluctantly I gave in to the fact that Jean was a winner and allowed him to court me. I even changed my bus route and, with the pretext that Sylvia needed supervision, abandoned Kiki in the hope of meeting Jean on Madison Avenue.

I now became a part of his entourage, a group of boys. One was the grandson of Matisse, the other of the Russian actor Georges Pitoeff. Their fathers spoke no English and were therefore out of work. Still another was the son of the composer Vittorio Rieti, who had written ballets for Diaghilev. All of us were affected by these fathers who had been part of history but were now cultural immigrants. We talked about them at first, but less and less. The strange no-man's-land in which they lived in the midst of New York was no more isolated than the expatriate school we attended, in which even the English classes, with their focus on the Romantic poets, had little connection with the American language of the streets.

It was Jean, with his gift for adventure, who organized our days. Like his friends, I became dependent on his magnetism. We formed a soccer team on which I played goalie in the park, and we walked across the Queensboro Bridge in the rain or made campfires in the snow on Sheep's Meadow. For these boys I smuggled into class my father's beer, which they drank behind raised desktops. I snuck them into my room in the apartment where my father pursued his difficult work, for he had to replenish the wallet so imprudently reduced before our landing.

But Father's work was making strange digressions. After the fall of France, he painted murals all over the apartment, this time not of long-haired dancing girls, flute players, and farm horses, the celebration of the gay peasant world I was accustomed to, but of apocalyptic visions of doom executed with feverish intensity. The Polish eagle, looking more like a plucked chicken, flew along the dining room wall with an arrow through its head, croaking "QUID QUID QUID EST VERITAS"; in the hallway a monstrous mule with four hands instead of hooves trampled a naked female body; in the study helmeted soldiers, their mouths full of huge teeth, lurked fearfully behind stumps of ruins. On either side of a wall lamp were the long-nosed, double-chinned profiles of himself and Mother, surveying the havoc with middle-aged melancholia.

I was vaguely embarrassed by these outpourings and tried to hurry my friends past them, but they observed the murals critically. "Hmm," they said. "Surrealism, I suppose." Jean murmured, "They remind me of the murals in the Russian Tea Room," which was not meant as a compliment.

That winter there began to be a lot of talk about money. It dawned on me that we were probably poor, but what that meant was not always clear. The piano and ballet lessons for which I longed were too expensive; on the other hand, entertaining was considered essential. "The more you spend, the more you make," said Mother, and, "If you start skimping, you're lost," and, "It's bad business to appear poor." And so we gave the impression of being rather better off than my new friends, who had arrived in the States without furniture or silverware, with barely a suitcase. Jean lived in a one-room apartment with his mother, an accomplished violinist, who supported him by playing in the orchestras of Broadway musicals. He would confide such details to me during rare moments of melancholy after long afternoons of rambling in the park, and I would feel sorry for him. But though my father was in contact with American architects and, with his growing command of the English language, had an air of self-assurance, he, too, looked like a troubled refugee when alone in his studio. His brow had grown furrowed, his cheeks sagged. He now painted his self-portrait looking like an aging Rembrandt, with a wild halo of graying hair and brooding eyes.

More and more my classmates and I escaped from our parents' world and lived in the park, made excursions to Bear Mountain and to an abandoned estate we had discovered on Long Island, the Mackay place in Roslyn. We kept house there for a whole weekend, having told our parents we were staying with a friend. We sat all night by the huge Renaissance fireplace singing the songs of Charles Trenet, burning stacks of old *Life* magazines, cooking potatoes in the embers. I thought of my mother and her fourteen Italian boyfriends during the other war. I, too, would probably remember this night as one of the most exhilarating in my life.

Back in New York, I noticed that Sylvia was never home anymore. Alarmed, I asked my mother at what time she returned at night.

"Oh, three o'clock, sometimes two."

"How do you know?"

"I try to wait up for her." She looked a bit sheepish, as if she too had been delinquent. "Do you suppose I should forbid her to go out so late?" I, who had just spent the night in an abandoned house with six boys, was indignant at

Sylvia's behavior. After all, she was only thirteen and had, I now noticed, become precociously alluring. Her brown hair had grown long, and around her neck she wore a black velvet ribbon with a brooch, which I considered provocative. Her lips were painted a bright red and she answered our questions with expert evasiveness. "We listened to music," she said, or, "We worked on our Latin," but mischief lurked in her dark eyes and I now began to worry about her. Wasn't she, after all, my responsibility? And my father, had I not neglected him, abandoned him to that lonely struggle of his?

I could hear him, in a rare mood of optimism, whistling an intricate contrapuntal tune that wandered on and on, rather like Bach's well-tempered clavichord, an endless variation on a theme, and this cheerful sound set my mind at ease. Yet only a few hours later, he once more lay in a miasma of self-pity on the purple striped couch bought on Columbus Avenue. I could hear the complaining strains of his voice rising and falling monotonously while Mother listened patiently and suggested remedies. "Should I ask the Huxleys for another loan?" she'd ask, knowing she could count on her oldest sister's generosity. But his debts to her humiliated Father. He did not want to make windows ever again; he wanted to paint, but he had to support us, his family. Life was so expensive, where did the money go? If only he could paint undisturbed he could be a success, he repeated endlessly. He could be as famous as the Surrealists who had arrived from Paris, the ones exhibited at the Museum of Modern Art. He was a middle-aged failure, a good-for-nothing. He might as well jump in the river.

"Don't be ridiculous," said Mother matter of factly, but he rushed out, slamming the door while I, falling on my knees in my room, prayed to God to keep him from the Hudson River. In tears I ran down to the kitchen where Mother was calmly cleaning out a china closet.

"What shall we do?" I cried. "What if he doesn't come back?"

"He probably went to the bar on the corner to have a beer."

"Then why does he frighten us like this?"

"He's having a hard time," she answered with a shrug and continued arranging her dishes, hanging up the cups, taking a step back to look at the effect. Yet she, too, looked tired and lonely; she, too, needed attention.

And how about Kiki? I had been avoiding my Belgian friend with the large, loose mouth, the sturdy legs, the sheepish devotion, all these months.

"What have I done?" she had asked pleadingly at first. "Why aren't we friends anymore?" Lately she had merely looked subdued. A poor student, she seemed to under-stand nothing, lost her books, sat in class as if she were absent. What was happening to her?

The morning after Father's outburst, determined to find out how Kiki was, I took the Eighth Avenue bus, as in the old days, but she did not get on at Eighty-sixth Street and did not come to school.

It was a day in late April, and once more spring had suddenly overtaken us. Central Park was soft and tender; the air hot, misty, and still. It was so surprising and exhaust-ing that we were all overcome by it as with a disease. We stood limply in the school courtyard, peeling off sweaters, unbuttoning, rolling up sleeves, leaning into the sun as if it were a drug. Two years had passed since Kiki and I had gone together on the bus and our countries had been invaded. "My father says it will be worse for Jews," she had said then. "He says that for us Jews this is only the begin-ning." On this day Jean, his skin glowing in the sun, leaned over me with a proprietary air. "Let's go rowing," he said. "But don't tell anyone. I'm tired of the gang."

And of course I met him as he had requested, furtively, by the reservoir. Hand in hand, we walked to the lake where he insisted on paying for the rowboat we rented, for he was proud. "You sit over there and I'll row," he ordered. His hands came toward me with the oars, then pulled back, over and over, and each time they approached I longed to kiss them. "What are you looking at?" he said, with that taunting smile of his.

"Nothing," I said, and blushed, for I had been watching his body so close to mine. Then, daring me, he exclaimed, "It's hot!" and took off his shirt. "I think I'll go swimming, shall I? What do you think?"

"No," I cried in alarm. "The water's filthy, and besides, it's forbidden."

"Do you never do what's forbidden?" he teased. "Are you always so well-behaved?"

"This is silly," I frowned. "You're just trying to provoke me." He took off his shoes and socks, looking me straight in the eye. He began to unbuckle his belt and I panicked. "If you do this, I'll pretend I don't know you."

A couple of sailors were rowing their girls alongside us. Jean waved at them. "Nice weather!" he called out. They waved back and rowed on, disappearing under a Japanese bridge.

"Now," he said, pulled off his pants, and dove in, tipping the boat dangerously. I took his seat and rowed away fast, hearing him come up snorting behind me. *"Méchante!"* he called. "Wait for me, it's all mud. I'm drowning in mud."

The sailors reappeared below the bridge, approaching us. "Help," cried Jean. "She threw me in." I slowed down enough to let him catch up and, after swimming frantically for a while longer, he caught the gunnel and climbed aboard, his legs black with mud, dripping and covered with dead leaves and algae. *"Méchante!"* he scolded again, dripping water on my neck, stepping over me to sit facing me, his shorts clinging to his body. "You traitor, you *vilaine*," he teased, still smiling. Then he leaned over me, grabbed the oars, and, laying them in the bottom of the boat, embraced me. He was wet and slimy, and I wiggled and screamed and fought myself out of his grip. "I have to go home! Get dressed."

"Why?" He dried himself with his shirt and pulled on his clothes.

"I have to call Kiki," I said.

"Kiki? The girl with the big mouth?"

"She's my friend," I protested crossly.

"You haven't been her friend in months. Kiki, Kiki, what a silly name. Wasn't she called Rosenberg? Isn't that her last name?"

"Yes," I said. He now looked puzzled and frowned.

"I read about a man called Rosenberg this morning in the papers. He threw himself from an eighth-floor window."

"She lives on the eighth floor! What street was it? West Side?"

He nodded slowly. "I'm pretty sure," he said. "Eighty-fourth, Eighty-sixth?"

"I have to go home! You'd better leave me off here."

"I wouldn't go there now," he said. "There's nothing you can do now. The man killed himself."

"I must see my father," I said, and without looking back ran past the fountain and across Sheep's Meadow into our street, where horses were lining up with their riders to enter the park. I let myself into the apartment, and inhaling the reassuring smell of cigar, sighed with relief. I could hear him rinse his brush, swishing it in water, tapping it against the side of the glass. Cautiously I opened the studio door and stood watching him as he tilted his head, lifted his arm, and began to color the sketches for windows tacked to his drawing board.

"Clairette!" he said when he noticed me.

"You're making windows again?"

"It's a big commission."

"Then you don't mind?"

"It's what I do best," he said.

"I wondered if you'd teach me."

He seemed overjoyed. Within ten minutes he had me installed at a drawing table with a fine charcoal pencil. "Start with a tulip," he said, and dutifully I began to copy the single flower he had set up for me, the delicate shading, the veins in the petals, the rounded stem. It was taken for granted that very soon I would be assisting him. This was the one inheritance I was assured of, though I already suspected Sylvia of being more gifted, more daring. But on that spring afternoon we worked together in the quiet studio while, through the open window, we could hear those struggling voices of singers practicing their scales, the interrupted arpeggios of violinists, all reaching for a difficult and elusive perfection.

12
ROMANCE IN CONNECTICUT

"I think I'm not supposed to hear," cried Betsy from somewhere within the house, and that was the end of summer.

We sat on the porch steps of the country house and held our breath, Svet and I, horrified at what we had said aloud. At least it had not been I who had volunteered the information that Monsieur M. was Madame Jolas's lover. In fact, I had been incredulous, for really it had struck me as very unlikely.

"Why, everyone knows it. Even my father says so," Svet insisted.

"But she's old," I protested.

"Old people do it too, you know." Svet smiled knowingly. "Look at my father and Helen."

"But she's fat!"

And then the hurt voice from inside the dark room. "I think I'm not supposed to hear." We ran inside and put our arms about Betsy, Madame Jolas's daughter, who was sitting at the piano in silence for once, but it was a kind of Judas kiss, for the harm had been done and could not be repaired.

We had betrayed them all: Madame Jolas, who had taken us to her voluminous, kindly bosom; Betsy, the friend whose straightforwardness and dedicated talent we admired more than anyone's; and dear, ghostly, vague Mr. Jolas. Now I could no longer stay under their hospitable roof. That evening, though September was just beginning and the night was filled with a tremendous pulsing of insects — an intoxicating sound of wildness and abundance that made my head reel with happiness — I called my parents in New York to tell them that Sylvia and I were returning to the city.

Svet, oddly enough, acted as if nothing had happened. She shrugged her shoulders when I mentioned my embarrassment. *"Une bêtise,"* she said. "After all, it's a compliment to Madame, no?" She would stay on until the first day of school with her father and Helen, his mistress, as if nothing had happened.

Maria Jolas was large and generous. She wore ballooning dresses with V necklines and picture hats with flattened roses on them. She had undertaken to make all of us exiled adolescents, as well as the entire Free French Navy, feel at home in the United States. In fact, one undertaking was helped along by the other, for during the winter months I had gone with other girls from the *lycée* to dance with the sailors for whom she had founded the canteen La Marseillaise. Flirtation was limited to the exchange of a kiss for a red pompom, and some of the boys from Brittany were so short they barely came up to our shoulders, but their costumes were becoming and they had respectful manners, calling us *"mesdemoiselles."* It was always an honor to be asked to dance by one of the black sailors from Martinique or Guadeloupe, for they were haughty and dignified. *"J'aime à revoir ma Normandie,"* sang a handsome sailor with a beautiful voice, his right hand on his heart, until he choked on his own tears.

We danced *valses musettes*, tangos, and *pasodobles*, and if the midnight curfew seemed too early, a sailor who had become my favorite partner would take me to a nightclub where we danced till dawn. He was a smooth dancer, and we were so attuned to each other's movements that when we danced the floor would clear. The international crowd of servicemen and their girls made way to watch us, and when the music stopped they clapped. He blushed, then asked me to marry him. "My father has a store in Honfleur," he assured me. "It will support us."

It was such an honorable proposal that I did not want to hurt his feelings. "I'm too young," I said lamely, though I was by then all of seventeen, wondering whether we could simply dance together through life.

Then in the spring, the French fleet had sailed off to North Africa and Madame Jolas's attention focused on her daughters, Tina and Betsy, and on us expatriate *"mesdemoiselles,"* their classmates at the *lycée*. She telephoned my parents and told them I was looking peaked and needed fresh air, that she would take me to her country house where Betsy would spend the summer months practicing the piano. But how about Claire's little sister, my mother asked? As if I were tied to her like a Siamese twin! And so Sylvia was invited too, and Betsy's friend Svet and Svet's friend Aniuta, who was recuperating from pneumonia.

Here in the Connecticut hills our life had centered around the lake, which was black and muddy and said to be inhabited by snakes. Its shores were a wild tangle of trees and vines. When we explored them in our rowboat, we imagined we were the first to come upon them, like Paul and Virginie. On the opposite shore, a considerable distance away, the hills were cultivated, and behind Madame Jolas's house there was a farm with a red barn and corn and hay fields. But even this landscape was strangely free-form, its unfenced fields and lawns joining houses with undefined borders or property lines. These homes, which sat slightly aslant on the land rising away from the lake, were shapeless as dowagers, and the spreading porches, kitchen wings, and little shacks behind them were full of flowerpots and broken furniture. The house rented by the Jolases had been empty for several years, and it was run down, full of chiming clocks grown rusty and hoarse with winter dampness.

Madame heaved painfully in the summer heat, her dresses a diaphanous gray or mauve. Mr. Jolas, a sweet, distracted gentleman of literary persuasion, who had been friends with Gertrude Stein, James Joyce, and Scott Fitzgerald, wandered disconsolately through the Connecticut countryside carrying a gallon bottle of wine. He too was a culturally misplaced person, rooted in that Paris of the thirties that to me had seemed such a nightmare. Perhaps life had come to an end for him, but for Madame Jolas it obviously had not. She believed in the future and was a staunch supporter of de Gaulle, firing us with her enthusiasm so that we wore the Cross of Lorraine pinned to our shirts.

Mr. Jolas tended the clocks. The oldest daughter, Betsy, was a single-minded musician with a determined lower jaw. When she sat at the piano, pounding away with strong hands, nothing could distract her except the jangling clocks, which, never synchronized, continually announced time when it least mattered. Then she slammed the doors of her little studio porch to shut them out, cursing savagely. There was something Wagnerian about her classical profile and long blond hair pulled back and falling heavily, like a horse's mane, behind her.

Betsy filled us with creative zeal and a sudden preoccupation with "our careers." We began to worry about which of the arts we would espouse and where our greatest talents lay, which caused some jealousies, since at least three of us considered ourselves painters. Tina and Sylvia mumbled that I was "too academic," since I painted from nature rather than rendering wild imaginings in Fauve colors. But seeing Betsy work endless hours at her piano, we set up a schedule of our own, painting in the morning, reading and writing verse in the early afternoon. Toward evening we swam or boated and sang rounds that echoed across the calm lake. After dinner it was time for theatricals, or, if Madame Jolas was home, we gathered around her to hear her sing the songs from Louisiana where she was born. Then, his face suddenly appearing in a darkened window, Mr. Jolas would observe us like a prowler and Betsy, capturing him with two arms about his neck, would drag him into our circle of light, crying, "I caught you, Daddy. Now you've got to stay with us." Grinning, he would sit down a moment, silent in a dark corner with his unruly gray hair, looking like the aging Beethoven.

Then he would vanish again as he had appeared.

Toward the middle of July, Svet's father, Mr. Alexeïeff, came with Helen, his mistress, to supervise us while Mr. and Mrs. Jolas returned to New York. Now everything changed in a subtle way. A wiry, dapper man with tightly curling brown hair, flaring nostrils, and a youthful physique, Mr. Alexeïeff had a passion for lecturing youth and expounding his ideas. He had left his wife behind "to the Germans," as Svet put it bitterly, and now the rather pale but devoted Helen, of a wealthy Chicago family, ministered to him and confirmed his own belief in his genius by admiring him boundlessly. Svet, after her first disillusionment, had decided to make the best of the situation, but had become cynical and loved to poke holes in the youthful idealism of the rest of us.

After dinner we sat around the table, a captive audience, and listened to Mr. Alexeïeff. He reasoned very systematically. "Assuming that," he would say. "The conclusion being . . . it is therefore evident that . . . , which is what we set out to prove."

Only Betsy had the courage to challenge him. "I don't agree at all!" she argued. "It doesn't make any sense."

"How interesting," he taunted. "Can you tell me why not?"

"Why! Why! I don't *like* it, that's why!"

"Emotional," he would say with a quiver of his faunlike nostrils. "Betsy is emotional. I respect that." In fact, he became more and more interested in Betsy. Whenever we went swimming in the afternoon, bursting with long-suppressed energy, doing somersaults and cartwheels on the lawn, taking running jumps off the diving board or having naval jousts riding on floating logs, Mr. Alexeïeff appeared. He wore a tiny bathing suit called *un slip*, a black rubber bathing cap over his curly hair, and a nose clip, a ridiculous object, to protect his sinuses. He would sit and stare at us or, suddenly meddlesome, organize us into swimming races or diving contests. But rather than competing with each other, we dissolved into silly fits and hysterical giggles, spouting mouthfuls of muddy lake water, dripping and slippery with wet hair and water lily leaves. Then Mr. Alexeïeff, exasperated by our lack of cooperation, lost his temper and shouted crossly, "That's enough nonsense." Defeated, he would retreat to the house, where Helen could pacify him by saying, "But they're only children . . ." while our laughter echoed over the lake.

One night, as we flitted about our bedrooms in diaphanous nightgowns, Svet, pink-cheeked and grinning in the crooked, insinuating way she had, announced, "You know, my father says Betsy has a splendid body."

Betsy bristled. "Is that so!" Her lower jaw set, tossing her blond mane over her shoulder, she went into one of the brooding moods that intimidated us. We retired to our beds, watching her storm off to her studio porch, where she lit two candles, closed the door, and began to play. She played and played, Chopin and Beethoven, then Honegger and Schönberg, in that vigorous way of hers, emotional but never sentimental, until she finally stopped and we heard only the moths and beetles fluttering against the screen.

For some reason, Mr. Alexeïeff seemed to dislike me. "She's pretty like a movie star," he would say, meaning, I could tell by his tone of voice, boringly pretty, uninteresting, and probably stupid. I also overheard him say, "I used to think she was intelligent when she was still shy." At ease among these girls, whom I considered my friends, I had lost my reticence and chattered like the rest of them. But it was not until Jean and his friends arrived that Mr. Alexeïeff's annoyance with me exploded, though I had in no way encouraged them to come. It was Svet, engaging in a little intrigue, who had given them our address. Now they were on their way, with a tent and pots and pans for camping outside the house. Every day I got an ardent note from Jean as they advanced through the suburbs of Westchester County, where they camped on a millionaire's lawn, and up through Connecticut, their feet getting sore and their socks moldy. "But this suffering is nothing," Jean wrote, "when I think that in a few days I'll clasp you in my arms!"

Oh dear, I thought, being as afraid of love as of an erupting volcano. I had been perfectly happy without it all these weeks, innocently in love with vines, cornstalks, and insects, with climbing roses and cherry trees, and with the black bottom of Lake Waramaug.

"Svet," I said, "You must warn your father. After all, you invited them."

"But we'll pretend they just came by chance. They have their tent. They can stay in the woods."

I began to look up the road toward the south with a mixture of dread and impatient longing. On the day they were expected, the wind began to blow, tugging at trees and shutters, banging the kitchen and bedroom doors. Finally the rain came, splattering on the dry road and the restless surface of the lake. We all gathered in the house, playing records of Charles Trenet, Sylvia and Aniuta arguing over the table space on which to stretch out their paper and finally spilling paint pots on the floor. At this point Mr. Alexeïeff's nerves gave way and he came storming into the room to demand silence. "This place sounds like a kennel full of mad dogs," he said with barely controlled rage. "I'm trying to think."

It was then that I spotted three bedraggled creatures rounding the bend of the road, packs on their backs, dripping in the downpour. My heart beat with uncontrolled leaps and I held my breath. If only Mr. Alexeïeff would disappear again to his upstairs room, to his art books and manuscripts, we might sneak the boys in somewhere and hide them in a cabin in the back. But he lingered and marched up and down the room, under the illusion that his presence soothed us.

I motioned to Svet behind his back, pointing at the road. "Look who's there," she exclaimed treacherously. "Why, Claire, it's your friend Jean!" Going out on the porch, she began to wave and call, "What a surprise!" I blushed under Mr. Alexeïeff's questioning glance. He was able to raise an eyebrow higher than anyone I'd seen before. Jean, in knee-pants, his blond hair sticking in wet curls to his forehead, now looked past Svet and saw me frozen to the spot. He crossed the porch, opened the door, and stood before me in a dripping pool. "You're sunburned," he said without smiling and touched my face gingerly with his hand, as if he were afraid the brown would come off.

"I think you should introduce me," said Mr. Alexeïeff. The two other boys, one a child of about ten with a freckled face, the other a sullen, swarthy fellow, had dropped their bags on the porch and Svet brought them in proudly.

"They walked all the way from New York, Papa!"

"And who's the decoy?" Mr. Alexeïeff looked at his daughter and at the two young men, then at me, face averted, hiding behind my hair. But he smiled graciously and welcomed them, shook hands and began to talk about his own youth and his own walking trips to visit a girl he had known in Moscow who had left for the Ukraine. Svet lit a fire and Betsy made tea. Behind Mr. Alexeïeff's back, Jean took my hand and squeezed it while exclaiming politely, "From Moscow to the Ukraine! That must have taken you more than a month!"

Mr. Alexeïeff arranged everything. The boys would stay for dinner and sleep on the sofas until tomorrow, when the rain could be trusted to stop. Jean and his friend Fabio were given brandy in their tea, and the little boy, Claudie, was made to strip and put on Aniuta's blue jeans and shirt. His teeth clattered on his teacup. Mr. Alexeïeff was a charming host, though he monopolized the conversation and slapped Jean on the shoulder, calling him *mon vieux* as if they were old buddies.

The following day, when the boys had gone up the mountain to set up camp under the damp trees, Claudie was sent down to me as a messenger with a little note. He found me behind the house, where I was sitting in an apple tree improvising on my recorder. When I jumped down from the tree, he put out his hand to caress my arm.

"I can't wait to see you alone," said the note. "Follow Claude and he will bring you to me."

The boy smiled, revealing a gap between his front teeth. "He is smart, your Jean," he said. "He is paid to be my tutor and so he brings me here, where he can be with you and I can run errands for him."

"Is that what he is supposed to be, your tutor?"

"Yes . . . ." The child seemed very worldly for his age.

"And the other boy, who is he?"

"Fabio owns the tent. He's bright, always doing geometry in his head. But they fight a lot."

"Why?"

Claudie raised his shoulders and smiled again. "Fabio didn't want to come here, but I don't mind. You have eyes like Michelle Morgan."

I was flattered and, giving him my hand, followed him up the hill. Behind the upstairs window I thought I saw Mr. Alexeïeff watching us.

I felt ambivalent about being summoned to see Jean like this. Should I obey? I wanted to see him, but was also afraid of him, as if he had become the mountain itself, a huge obstacle on the horizon. How autocratic of him to wait up there while we scrambled through what was probably poison ivy, a weed we had heard much about but did not yet know how to identify. Was he watching us through the leaves with that ironic, triumphant smile of his? And how about Fabio, who resented having had to come here because of me?

Jean lay in the tent like a pasha, smoking his pipe. He hardly looked up when we arrived. "You know what I told you, Claudie. Beat it."

"Okay, okay," said the child and, grinning at me, vanished. I heard him thrashing down the hill again and stood, disconcerted, in the entrance of the low tent.

"Aren't you going to sit down?" asked Jean, and I did so obediently.

"Where is Fabio?" I asked.

"He went to the village to buy provisions. We are alone." He turned to me, leaning on one elbow, scowling.

"Fabio obeys you, too?"

"Are you surprised?" His smile was ironic and made me shy. We were alone among the trees, hidden from the rest of the world by an impenetrable green maze, and Jean's mood was foreign to me.

"What's the matter with you?" I asked him.

"I'm jealous. Down there with your friends you're very cold to me, you don't need me at all." This seemed so complicated a statement that I was incapable of defending myself, and so I leaned over and kissed him, rather brazenly I thought. But he still looked sullen, his full lower lip pouting, his huge blue eyes cold. "You only love me for my *beaux yeux*," he had told me once, and there was some truth in this, for to me his eyes were the most beautiful in the world.

"And that Mr. Alexeïeff, he's some kind of pervert," he added petulantly. "He likes little girls. I saw him look at your friend Betsy and positively drool."

"Well, he doesn't like me, so you don't have to worry about that."

He resumed his smoking, staring at the peak of the tent above him in silence, and I sat there, my hands crossed primly in my lap, counting the pairs of socks that hung drying on one of the tent lines.

"You're not very friendly today," I said.

"No," he said. "You'd better go down again."

What nerve! He had summoned me and let me kiss him. Now he was sending me down the mountain again, without anything, without . . . what we had done without occurred to me only dimly.

"All right," I said. "I'll go." And not looking back I stood up, dignified, smoothing down my pale blue shorts and brushing back my hair with a shrug.

"It'll pass." He waved his pipe, satisfied no doubt that he had taught me some complicated lesson in submissiveness. "I get these moods. Don't pay any attention." But as I walked away with as much poise as possible, I could feel his cold eyes on my back. Angry, I began to run. When I reached the field that led to the house, I saw Mr. Alexeïeff coming toward me with a pinched look.

"I want to talk to you," he said. "Certain things must be clarified. I cannot be held responsible for what goes on between you and that young man of yours, you understand? And since you use these devious tactics for attracting men, you will be in charge of their entertainment in a more practical manner. You shall cook the dinner tonight. I hope you are capable of it."

"But it was Svet who invited them!"

"It is quite evident that you are the lure, my dear." His waspish severity intimidated me so that again I ran away and climbed back into the apple tree, where it felt safe and secret, and wept with confusion at the strange behavior of the male.

Cooking dinner turned out to be simpler than expected, for no one came down from the mountain all day. The following morning Mr. Alexeïeff and Helen returned to the city. He had called Madame Jolas and complained. "The task of watching these children has become too complicated for me," he said. "I was never meant to be a chaperone."

In the afternoon Jean paid us a gracious visit, all smiles, surrounded by his retinue. He put his arm around my shoulders, which I took as a sign that I had been forgiven for my supposedly cold behavior. The sun had come out and the lake was a glassy blue. We swam and had sea jousts and boated to what we called the Island, a wild peninsula full of singing birds. When Madame Jolas arrived from New York after dinner, we were all once more dressed in clean, ironed clothes and looked like model youths, sitting on the porch and cheering as she descended with awkward bundles from the taxi followed by her gentle husband, a foot shorter than she. A tall man in a pink shirt whose sleek, graying hair was parted in the middle followed and was introduced to us as Mr. M.

I felt sorry for Svet, for the welcome we gave the Jolases was much warmer than the subdued farewell that had accompanied her father on his way. Poor Svet went to bed early, claiming a headache, while the rest of us gathered around Madame, who sat down, with her guitar, in a straw armchair on a pile of records, which broke into small pieces under her huge weight. We laughed at her confusion and begged her to sing. "The waiters went to and to and fro, in that elegant old chateau."

Mr. M. sang a song about twelve thieves all dressed in white. Then Jean sang about "the girls of St. Malo," Fabio sang about "the girls of La Rochelle," and I sang "Old maid will you dance, and I shall give you an egg." Then we all sang about a coconut merchant in Marseilles and another one about a Flemish troubadour.

"Bravo," cried Mr. M., and we decided he was all right, for he sang well and we had heard of him as a poet of the thirties who had helped found the Surrealist movement.

Finally we were silenced by the stars and the crickets. Madame Jolas yawned and got up to retire, but Jean lingered awhile, sending Claudie up the mountain with Fabio. Behind the toolshed where it smelled of honeysuckle, he kissed me and said I tasted like the lake. The moon, which had come up pink and hazy, signaling heat for tomorrow, was reflected in his eyes. Madame Jolas called his name from the front porch and he went to her promptly across the lawn, raising his eyebrows in anticipation of a scolding, but she only told him that since she knew he was a gentleman, she trusted him entirely.

"She's a very nice woman," he said with an amused smile when he returned to me. "She told me, '*C'est très gentil tout ça!*' You see, she gives us her blessing." As we parted, he toward the mountain and I toward the house, we turned back several times to wave at each other, for the moonlight was like a web about us, keeping us in its spell.

When I returned to the room I shared with Betsy, I noticed that she had drawn all the shades, a thing she had never done before. As I entered she dropped the book she had been reading, the third volume of *Jean Christophe*, muttering, "It's terribly late!" Then she covered her head with the sheet. It was stifling in the room, and I turned off the light and opened the shades again. At the edge of the field Jean was standing motionless, looking at our window. Raising his arm he waved one last time and disappeared among the trees.

During the next four days, Jean and I pretended to be a married couple, walking arm in arm on the street of the village. We bought a vile bottle of Marsala at the liquor store, convincing the proprietor of our advanced age. We drank it at a picnic after a long hike on a sweltering day, in a meadow full of cows, a mock wedding feast at which Svet took photographs of Jean kissing me. Aniuta announced her engagement to Fabio and was in turn photographed nestling in his arms. Unfortunately, in the midst of this bacchanalia, I insisted that Sylvia was too young to drink. Furious, she walked off alone and disappeared along the road. We paid no attention at first and began to wash each other with watermelon rinds until Betsy, who had remained annoyingly sober, frowned and got up, muttering, "This is idiotic! Sylvia will get lost," and went to rescue her.

By now the bottle was empty and our heads had begun to pound. As we dozed in each other's arms, Claudie having laid his reeling head on Svet's bosom, the cows suddenly came marching toward us with slow determination. We gathered our knapsacks in a hurry and ran, for Svet insisted that one of them was a bull.

The empty asphalt road melted under our feet and the hazy sun was like a hammer over our heads. Jean stopped by the roadside and threw up neatly in the ditch, after which he assured us he felt much better, but we no longer trusted anyone's sense of direction. The lake on our right should somehow have been on our left, and hills seemed to repeat themselves, monotonously similar. Svet and Jean began to quarrel.

"We were all friends until you came," said Svet. "You think you're the boss, but only Claire is dumb enough to let herself be pushed around."

"You're just jealous," said Jean, "because you're too cross-eyed for anyone to fall in love with." Since Svet had one eye that wandered off in odd directions, this was cruel.

"You think you're irresistible!"

"You're so cross-eyed you can't even tell a bull from a cow."

Not wanting to face the evidence that Jean had a sadistic streak, I began dreaming of the North Sea. If only I knew the way to the ocean I would be able to go home again, I thought.

We ended up going in opposite directions: Svet, Aniuta, Tina, and Fabio south; Jean and I, with Claudie holding onto my hand, north. We talked of moving into an abandoned house on a hill with closed shutters, a well, and raspberry bushes. With Jean I would become a pioneer in Connecticut and forget about the North Sea. We would plant corn and I would make bread and our memories of Europe would be overgrown with honeysuckle and bittersweet.

A farmer in a field had told us to keep walking "straight into the sun," and as the sun began to sink we wondered if we should keep following it beyond the horizon all the way around the world. Finally the raft and the rowboat and the cottage itself came into sight. Walking toward us were the four others. They had rounded the lake in the opposite direction.

Jean never called me back to the seclusion of his tent, and his black mood did not return until the night before he and his two friends were to leave for New York. We were walking together on a lonely road that smelled of asphalt, high on a hill, when he began to pout. Jean's lower lip was full and strongly marked. With his straight nose, muscular back, and large, strong hands, and his wide eyes, which gave him an incongruous look of childish innocence, he seemed to me of a classical perfection. Now his pout was spectacular. Swallows were streaking by us, their wings collapsing like arrows. Otherwise it was alarmingly still. Even our footsteps were cushioned in the soft asphalt.

"What is the matter?" I asked. I was afraid that in this mood he might commit suicide, or join de Gaulle's army, or drink a whole bottle of whiskey and get sick.

"When I'm gone you'll be happy, you and your friends," he said. "You will be able to take yourselves seriously again and do all your artistic work. I'm just a disturbance in your summer."

I assured him of the contrary, that without him I would pine away, and yet I knew there was truth in what he said. With him I thought only of the present, I lived from day to day. When he was gone I worried about the life ahead for which I must be prepared. "Work is the only thing that makes one happy," my mother always said, and inspired by Betsy, we had all taken ourselves seriously that summer until Jean came.

We turned back to the house swatting at gnats in silence. In the distance we could hear Betsy playing her piano with suppressed fury, as if music could drown out the distractions of summer's romance. I imagined her sitting there in the candlelight with that angry frown of hers, the determined chin set, the strong hands pounding the keys.

The three boys left early the next morning and I cried in the apple tree, then dried my tears and went back to work. I drew a carefully shaded study of an ear of corn in its husk, with the blond silk spilling out of it, the shiny kernels in tidy rows gleaming between the leaves. It took me five days to finish. On the fifth day Sylvia made an enormous painting of a field of cornstalks turning into an army, each husk containing a grinning face; a black skeleton flew through the sky above the field. It took her exactly half an hour and was declared by Mr. Alexeïeff, who had returned to take us in hand now that the boys were gone, to be a work of genius. The result of my patient labor was considered academic and without imagination. "But that's all right," said Mr. Alexeïeff. "Claire is the marrying type."

I began to think that perhaps I was not an artist. Betsy shrugged when I explained my doubts to her. "Nonsense," she said. "At seventeen we are outgrowing the gifted child bit. Now comes the tedious acquiring of technique. Real originality comes afterwards." I knew that to these girls marriage was a fate worse than death, and only artistic fulfillment and fame among the avant-garde was a future worth looking for. They were taking their revenge on me for my romance with Jean. "After all," said little Aniuta, "you can't have everything," and suddenly it was always my turn to do the dishes or to iron my sister's dirndl skirts while the others went off to swim. Only Betsy seemed beyond jealousy.

"What will you do, Betsy, marry or have a career?" I asked.

"I certainly hope that one would not exclude the other," she said. "Look at my parents. They love each other, yet my mother has her own activities."

"And how," mumbled Svet. Betsy looked at her questioningly for a moment, then turned away. There was no telling what Svet might be implying with that insinuating smile of hers.

That evening after our swim I asked Svet what she had meant. We were sitting in wet bathing suits on the porch. Betsy had gone in ahead to change and it was then that Svet told me. "Why do you suppose Mrs. Jolas is always in New York while my father has to come and watch us? She has a lover and it's that Mr. M., the Surrealist poet."

"No," I said. "I don't believe it."

"You're so naive."

And so the summer ended and I returned to New York, where Jean was waiting for me at the fountain in Central Park. Whenever he summoned me, I went. I began to summon him myself. "Art," I thought, "who needs it?" I flitted about like a leaf, and Jean was the wind that drove me.

Until finally the trees were bare, and he no longer showed up at our rendezvous.

13
RINGS

Sophia Smith, founder of the college of my choice, must have been a redoubtable woman. She planted her campus behind the lacy screen of Grecourt Gate, a feminine camouflage for liberated minds. In January 1944 I entered Smith as a sophomore and began my true apprenticeship as an American. The Connecticut Valley was so wide that the horizon seemed infinitely distant in a continent of wasted spaces. In shapeless brick towns such as Northampton, whole populations of Poles, Greeks, Italians, and French Canadians cohabitated, but did not give it a homogeneous character.

The Smith girls, too, were a distinct breed, identifiable mostly by the quality of their flesh, which was of a good, firm consistency, pink and smelling of soap and Johnson's baby powder. Dressed uniformly in gray flannel Bermuda shorts, bobby socks, and lumber shirts, they displayed a vast expanse of smooth shank. All week long their hair was set in bobby pins, to be released suddenly on weekends to crown them with glory. Then, dressed in silk dresses, fur coats, little hats with veils, silk stockings, and high heels, they would fly off like gaudy birds of paradise in search of "men." Next to them I felt like a chicken — sallow, skinny, and unwholesome.

Smith girls became for me "the Americans," so that I tended to think of this country as inhabited only by women. "How friendly Americans are," I would think. "How generous. And how many cashmere sweaters they own." Even now, when I imagine cities where I have never been — Chicago, St. Louis, Cleveland — I people them with those same Smith girls, grown middle-aged, and their daughters, who are also Smith girls. I see them living in vast houses with closets full of pastel sheets and towels, and bathtubs full of lots of hot water — a population of Amazons playing bridge, discussing politics, getting drunk on cocktails, supporting the Red Cross, and discussing that other distant breed, the men, as if they were soldiers in barracks talking about whores.

I had been able to get a room to myself, in what was called the Quadrangle, a lovely place that echoed with singing voices and bicycle bells. I tried to pretend that it was a communal courtyard surrounded by the cottages of spinster ladies, and I a maiden *béguine,* safely removed from the turmoil of the outer world. I began to read Dostoyevski in unhealthy doses, moving during the course of one afternoon from the lower bunk of my bed to the upper bunk, then to the window seat in search of more light.

It was during one of these intense Russian evenings that a strange girl came to visit me. She had pale, shiny skin, a Dutch-boy haircut, the usual expanse of exposed thigh, and she began at once to tell me in a clinical way about her affairs with Amherst boys. In fact, she said, she had recorded them on paper for Creative Writing 21. Since I was an accomplished typist in need of pocket money, would I please type them for her?

She came to see me regularly to bring me new install-
ments, exposing me to the sordid details of "sex," a word I
had never heard before. Somehow *l'amour* was an
altogether different matter. Sex occurred in a semi-
conscious state of drunkenness, often in cars or in dorm
rooms that smelled of sweat socks and gym sneakers. The
danger of this grim sport was pregnancy, against which
various techniques, all totally incomprehensible to me,
were prescribed. If they failed, one could always get an
abortion. My new acquaintance offered to find me a blind
date, though Amherst was, during wartime, inhabited only
by 4Fs: tubercular, epileptic, and, I believed in my ignorance, blind. I protested vehemently that I was in no need
of dates, inventing elaborate excuses. Puzzled, my disturbing visitor left me to my books.

From Dostoyevski I moved on to Alain Fournier, with
whom I had a touching love affair in the stacks of the
library, reading his youthful letters and any other scraps of
information I could find about his short life. Thanks to the
inspired enthusiasm of several teachers, I then discovered
English literature: John Donne, Thomas Hardy, Christopher Marlowe, and the incredible Emily Brontë. The bony
language I was beginning to master was a precious gift, a
whole new dimension in my life, more hospitable, less
hermetic than French. I played with its words as with new
toys, and I too signed up for Creative Writing 21. In this
course I imagined that the rather fey gentleman who was
the supreme judge of our creativity became my friend. I
say imagined, for Robert Gorham Davis was as shy as I, so
that friendship with him became a silent understanding, an
unspoken sympathy, a tacit alliance between us against the
girl with the sex life. He encouraged me to write compositions in broken English, for which I have remained eternally grateful, and he invited me to his home, where he had
a wife and children, and where we discovered a mutual
passion for playing acting games such as charades and The

Game. Under the pretext of acting, we lost our inhibitions and did the most bizarre things, rolling around on the floor, jumping up and down on one foot, grimacing like rabbits or chimpanzees, wiggling like caterpillars.

At Mr. Davis's house I met another teacher of literature, a courtly poet who specialized in marrying Smith girls. Alfred Fisher had just terminated his fourth marriage at the time, and I spoke with him about French literature, which he knew well. When I mentioned having met him, however, a blond girl with a large, hungry mouth turned to me and said casually, "Oh, yes, he's divine. I'm trying to have an affair with him, too." Aghast, I quickly changed the subject. Was there something wrong with me, I wondered, that I shied away from this overt preoccupation with sex? Was the conception of *pudeur*, meaning a certain reserve and discretion, totally foreign to Americans? Were matters of the heart merely questions of a rather grim biology? Or was I, after all, a puritan?

Delegations visited me in my room, sympathetic but concerned about my lack of dates. Some of these girls were engaged, which meant they had diamond rings to hold up to the light for everyone to see. They had a special status, and were the aristocrats among us. They had "arrived," and could be heard endlessly discussing what color curtains they would buy for their living rooms and what pattern of silver they would demand as wedding presents but had never noticed the color of their fiancés' eyes. One night an alumna came to spend her wedding night in the guest room of the dormitory. Before the "consummation," she came upstairs, to show herself in her lace negligee, on the pretext of borrowing a hairpin, and the next morning she returned to describe the experience.

I hid from these disturbing intrusions in my room, where I had now become deeply involved with William Blake. Like him I fancied I had visions of huge angels that howled prophetic messages throughout the night. In a recurrent dream I was running over the surface of the earth, a desolate and charred place where dead trees stood gesticulating against flaming red skies. Under my feet the thin crust of the ground kept breaking away like brittle chocolate, and beneath it was a dark, gaping void. I had to run faster and faster to keep myself from falling into these holes and would wake up in the morning exhausted.

No wonder the thoughtful Smith girls worried about me. They decided I must cultivate popularity. My French accent had definite appeal but, they inquired, did I have "a line"? By this they meant a special way of bantering, a kind of conversational formula that would "keep the ball rolling." It would help if I smoked or drank, they added, but I, having been brought up on my father's precious, aged wine, thought whiskey a weird Anglo-Saxon aberration.

I was first put to the test at the canteen, where some servicemen were brought every Saturday to be entertained. Since the girls at the college outnumbered this small contingent of males, the dormitories took turns doing the honors. On our lucky Saturday we lined up at one end of a large room, all dressed in low-cut gowns except me, demure in a dirndl skirt and peasant blouse. At the opposite end of the room a door opened and a flock of frightened-looking sailors entered, dressed in their black uniforms. Like bulls let loose in a ring, they stood in clusters, undecided, while the girls examined them, displaying their imposing bosoms. Then the music began to play persuasively and I, in a mad moment of daring, plunged ahead and asked the first sailor I encountered to dance. Dancing did not frighten me. I knew I did it well, but whether the young man swung me too roughly or I had not used enough thread when sewing the hooks on my skirt, it promptly fell to the floor. There I stood, without even a slip, the garter belt holding up my silk stockings revealed.

The girls eyed me with disbelief. Had I planned this
striptease, or was I simply too awkward for words? The
sailor, dumbstruck, did not know how to react.

The situation was so bizarre I decided I had better
disappear, and picking up my skirt, I ran across the entire
campus back to my room. There, in the safety of my upper
bunk, I laughed hysterically. Poor little sailor, I thought,
remembering his anguished face.

My friends the Smith girls, discouraged by this first
clumsiness of mine, left me in peace for a while until, with
the advent of spring, it was time for the inevitable "House
Prom." Where to find enough men now became the prime
concern, for fiancés, past and potential, were at that
moment about to land in Normandy, but certain traditions
could not be broken. The world was so tense that the maps
in the papers seemed to crackle with static. Generous to a
fault, the girls made every possible effort to find me a
suitable date. "Just be yourself," they instructed me. "You're
cute enough. Just wear something sexy." And so I con-
sented to be a good sport and agreed to pay a huge sum
toward the lodging, liquor, and general entertainment of
an unknown medical student.

At the house meeting of the prom's planning committee,
the lack of an adequate place in which to entertain our
dates was deplored. The clubhouse, generally used for this
purpose, tended to be overcrowded with "necking" couples
every Saturday night, and someone suggested that a special
room with cubicles be built in the gym to afford couples
more privacy. The pros and cons of this were seriously
discussed and the idea was finally abandoned as being
rather too obvious, so we went to meet our contingent of
medical students on Saturday evening at a local restaurant.
Reluctant, I hung back, postponing the confrontation, only
to discover too late that every presentable gentleman had
been taken and the only one left was a pathetic, meager
young man with even less of a "line" than myself. There was

nothing else to do but sit down beside him and let the evening proceed. When everyone was drunk while I remained chillingly sober, we retired to the dormitory to change and reappeared in dazzling long gowns with white gloves and pearl necklaces. The lights in the downstairs parlor were dim; the music played softly. I was used to whirling to waltzes and dancing intricate, artful tangos with the French sailors, but here it was the thing to shuffle to slow foxtrots cheek to cheek, with arms intertwined, eyes glazed, and expression sensuous, the "smoother" boys singing the words suggestively in one's ear. Before I knew it, my tongue-tied partner had me firmly in his grip and, breathing heavily down my neck, was murmuring, "I wanna hug you."

I bolted. Stumbling over entwined forms, I ran up the stairs and locked myself in my room. Pleading delegations of girls assured me that I was being unkind to the poor young man, and no doubt I was, for he had merely done what was expected of him. But the convention seemed so barbaric that I remained in a hysterical panic behind my locked door all weekend. After that the girls gave up, deciding there was something wrong with me. I wondered if perhaps I was frigid or just too foreign to fit in, and yet should I give up the best education the United States had to offer a woman simply because I was unable to attend a prom? No, I refused to think of myself as a wallflower, a spoilsport, an unpopular girl whom no one would ask to a party, and by the following autumn I was ready to try a new approach.

Pinning the photographs of several handsome cousins to the walls of my room, I invented romances. To make things easier, an older man — he was probably all of thirty — whom I had met in New York during the summer began to bombard me with special-delivery letters. He was a glib advertising man with literary aspirations and I was not insensitive to his charms. He sent letters in verse typed in oversized script on huge pieces of paper, in patterns that wandered like garlands all over the page. These letters, full of poetic images and amorous innuendos, were just the thing to dazzle Smith girls.

Every morning the special-delivery boy arrived on his bicycle and, sitting on the porch steps, I would read the message to my audience. My image began to improve. The Smith girls wanted to know all about this man of experience and "how far I had gone." It was out of the question to admit that I had fled from his aggressive advances at our last meeting. For them I created a sophisticated world of refugee authors, composers, artists, parties in studios, superior intellectual relationships, and meetings in art galleries and at the ballet.

Every now and then I went home for the weekend to gather material. There I sat by the telephone and accepted invitations from various young and not-so-young men — officers on leave, Dutch marines, British fliers, an asthmatic actor, a limping art critic. With them I began to act out various romantic parts, usually the heroine of a French movie. One day I was Michelle Morgan dressed in a raincoat and beret, another day I was Danielle Darieux in *Mayerling*. Like a chameleon, I changed into whatever my escort imagined me to be, mostly some ethereal creature, an undine that would vanish at the first touch, and in fact the good-night kiss at the door of the apartment house, watched over by a discreet but observant doorman, was as far as these adventures went. Sometimes I imagined briefly that I had fallen in love, only to be soon disillusioned. Then there was the difficult problem of disentangling myself from a relationship that was becoming intolerable, and all this I did to satisfy the curiosity of the Smith girls. My image now was at least sophisticated, if rather eccentric and arty. Instead of going to proms, I wandered on weekends through the mountains with a bearded sculptor, a conscientious objector who lived in a cabin and cooked vegetarian stews on his coal stove. "He's not very clean," the girls said, wriggling their noses.

After two and a half years in college I walked in the procession of graduates, each of us dressed in virginal white, each carrying a long-stemmed American Beauty rose, and received a diploma. I'm not certain it made a Smith girl of me, for to my regret I have had little contact with any of them since. Every ten years I receive a communication from the alumnae association inviting me to a grand reunion and asking me all kinds of astonishing questions. "Do you and your husband sleep in a double or in twin beds?" "Do you and your husband wear pajamas at night?" "Does your husband wish for a reservation at the hotel while you stay with your classmates in the dorm?" It is as if they are trying to reduce my marriage once more to a blind date.

It must have been ten years after graduation that I was having dinner with friends in New York City's Chinatown, in a neighborhood not yet cleared of its derelict bums. The night was warm, and in the Bowery, where we walked after dinner, the sidewalks were strewn with the bodies of grizzled, decrepit men dressed in rags, some with vestiges of former respectability still clinging to them in the form of dirty business suits, stringy ties, frayed shirt collars. Some of the faces too had refined looks, as if these men had fallen so low because of some weakness, a gentleness of spirit unable to withstand the hardships of life. Most of them seemed asleep, dead drunk, bleary-eyed, snoring, but as I stepped over their outstretched legs, their eternally lived-in shoes, their crumpled pants, one of them raised his head, and seeing me, exclaimed in a mournful reproach, "Oh, you Smith girls!"

Profoundly shaken, I looked down at him, but it was not a face I knew. Either my education clung to me so visibly that I had become a stereotype, or the gesture of coolly stepping over the bodies of prostrate, broken males was typical of the average American female as personified by the Smith girl I had tried, at one time, to become.

14
CALIFORNIA

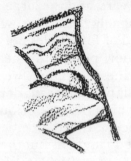

In the summer of 1946, my father returned to Europe to have an exhibition in Amsterdam. Mother, Sylvia, and I went west to visit Mother's family. Finally I would get to meet this oldest sister, Maria, and her famous husband, Aldous Huxley. Aunt Rose and Bonne Maman had found a refuge near them in California. So while Father returned to the past, we galloped with insatiable appetite all the way across America.

What space there was! What monotonous, hot, liberating mileage. We drove in an old wooden-bodied station wagon filled with my mother's statues. The excuse for this adventure was an exhibition of her work in the Beverly Hills Hotel, in a gallery run by Elizabeth Taylor's parents. Mother had enticed my latest boyfriend, Bobby White, to accompany us as codriver. She had done this one evening by wrapping herself in a white feather boa, something she had unearthed from a trunk. Oh, she had been irresistible, and I was well aware of it. It had nothing to do with me, or so it seemed at the time.

So there was Bobby, with his guitar, his cowboy boots, and his camper's knife at his belt. I traveled Route 66 in an amorous dream caused by his proximity in that creaking old car. It was loaded down with frail terra-cottas and tough bronze heads of various celebrities Mother had encountered through the years, and the large plaster figure called *Liberation* — all extremely breakable, which meant we were restricted to a speed of forty miles per hour.

Outside the window passed the steaming landscape of Pennsylvania. In Zanesville, Ohio, we blew a tire; on the banks of the Mississippi, dangerous derelicts heckled us. In Oklahoma the heat hit us with ferocious intensity. America was large but difficult. It did not beguile with touristic charms; it just went on and on. But the wealth of the space was enough to win us over. I felt as if I had been sitting on the edge of a tippy platter for the last six years and had finally found my equilibrium by reaching the middle.

In Taos, New Mexico, we spent a few days in a motel and visited the Huxleys' friend Frieda Lawrence, her Italian boyfriend, Angelino, and another eccentric personality called Brett, whose large hearing aid was studded with silver Indian decorations. Germanic, energetic, weighty Frieda urged us up the mountain heights to visit "The Chapel," a memorial to her famous husband, D. H., whose portrait my father had painted in the thirties. This chapel had been built by Angelino. He began to flirt in Italian with my mother as he drove us up there. All this, combined with D. H.'s pornographic paintings of flaming phalluses, his boots and hat left on the altar to be venerated, and the high altitude, made Bobby and me explode with nervous laughter. I kept wanting things to be proper and conventional in those days, and blushed at my mother's unmotherly behavior, her girlish manipulation of policemen, Indian chiefs, and motelkeepers, all of whom seemed to fall for her charms, taking us for three sisters with one common boyfriend. At night we all slept in one room, which I found shocking.

Whatever it was about Taos—Bobby's sudden need for a wild mare to ride through the orange desert, the enormous black sombrero he bought himself, the full moon on the barren landscape behind the motel—it was here that he asked me to marry him and I said yes, of course. It seemed quite logical that we should.

In Flagstaff we slept on the floor of a hotel lobby together with the cowboys and Navajo Indians who had all come to town for a rodeo to take place the following day. Then came terrifying barren stretches, infernos of stone. In Las Vegas, instant brides who had married their spouses at drive-in facilities sat forlorn, wearing corsages, in gambling joints. We crossed Death Valley at night with packs of dry ice and then, in the cool of the morning, arrived in the Mojave Desert, where a sign along the road announced YOU HAVE ARRIVED.

This was Aunt Rose's way of signaling the whereabouts of Pearblossom, a hamlet in which she inhabited a charming shack in the midst of dust and Joshua trees. Here Rose had ended her long flight from the Germans through the South of France and halfway across the world. Already she had made the desert bloom, having fed her three irises with coffee grinds, and had named every butte, as the elephantlike hills on the horizon were called. She had become Rose-of-the-Mojave, with a new husband and a new son. Now here I was with a new fiancé, leaving the trail of my new country behind me like a wedding veil. Everything had fallen into place, and Bobby and I decided to go no farther. The light in Rose's desert was enchanting and golden, like her skin and her voice. We adopted her. Mother and Sylvia drove on to join the Huxleys and Bonne Maman in the San Bernardino Mountains, half an hour's drive down the road.

There Maria had rented a nondescript cabin in the mountains for the summer. Behind it, Aldous worked in a silver trailer. Bonne Maman lived in another cabin with Rose's daughter, Olivia de Hauleville, a poetic child on whom everyone doted. We visited them regularly for long walks followed by tea. Though Rose was already quite rooted, Maria seemed to live in temporary quarters. She had few possessions, and it was hard to identify her with this landscape. She was thin, intense, elegant. I felt as if she expected total surrender to whatever it was she demanded, a loyalty I could not give her, for I was in love. I had seen her only briefly before, perhaps twice in my life, but I was in awe of her. Whenever she had been mentioned, it was understood that she was perfectionism, a leader to follow, as we all followed her now from coast to coast. No wonder her nickname was Coccola, or Coq, the little rooster, for short.

During the day, in the desert, I could see Rose looking repeatedly with an anxious frown through the bamboo trellis at her window toward the mountains in the West.

"What are you expecting?" I would say. "Who is coming from there?"

"I thought it was a gray Chevrolet. Coccola has a gray Chevrolet. When I see it I get cramps in my stomach."

Why, I wondered. What was Rose's fear? Then the day proceeded in its hot *dolce far niente,* lunch followed by a long nap, after which Rose donned her straw hat and we swam in a nearby pool. The air was so dry that we shivered as we emerged from the precious water. Sometimes we drove to the buttes and walked in this moonlike land.

Once a week, Rose and her new American husband, Billy Wessberg, drove to Lancaster to collect his unemployment check and shop for food. On those days lunch was gourmet—the thick, yellow cream from a nearby ranch poured over peaches grown in oasis orchards—and the mood expansive. This strange desert was a mixture of aridity and plenty, and Rose, with her sensuous gift for enjoying the moment, filled the day with song and laughter.

But during our frequent visits to the mountains, I became acquainted with Maria's demands, her perfectionism, her worried management of "the refugees" who had now become her responsibility, since she had persuaded them to join her. She had drawn us all to her like a magnet, and now that we were all near, what was she to do with us?

Aldous carried his distinguished, handsome head with apparent fatigue. It always leaned forward, as if it were leading his elongated, slack-kneed body during the long walks we took. I began to picture the thoughts that crowded his brain as extremely breakable eggs. He looked down at the ground with pale, half-seeing eyes as if he were reading thoughts along the mountain trails, always ruminating over subjects for his musical conversation — musical because the voice itself sang the sentences with an extremely British accent in this very un-British place. The terrifying challenge was to respond to all this thought, this endless information.

With my fledgling literary ambition, Maria "arranged" for me to walk by his side, to learn, to act intelligent. Instead I played naive, an easy way out. Were those blocks of salt left in the mountain meadows to make salted butter, I inquired? His upper lip curled then like that of a llama about to spit.

"Now, now, my dear." He'd pat me gently, patronizingly, but it was a smile after all. I had amused the sage, albeit with stupidity.

A walk by the side of Krishnamurti was more peaceful. He attended Maria's teas, vast family gatherings where she served homemade plum jams, exotic nectars, and perfumed maté, a South American tea, to her two sisters, her somewhat imperious mother, Aldous (playing the absentminded paterfamilias), "the girls," as Sylvia and I were called, and Rose's children. In our midst sat the gentle Hindu, who I was told was a saint of sorts, and who was urged to eat.

"Krishnaji forgets to eat," Maria would exclaim. "I counted the eggs in his refrigerator. He hasn't touched one in weeks." She fussed over him and he let it slide by. He simply *was,* which I found refreshing. And so I joined him on a day's walk. He was good at walking, elastic, supple, and kept silent so that we could concentrate on taking step after step. That day we climbed along a ridge higher than ever. "Once I followed a mountain lion a whole day and a night," he said. I would not have minded being that lion.

One afternoon Bobby fell asleep in a hammock, one hand on his heart, dressed in blue denim. All his life he has dressed in blue denim. Maria looked at him and said, "How beautiful he is, like a Picasso." I loved her for this and knew that her role was a difficult one, that of generosity and responsibility. She knew that Bobby, who was a sculptor, had no more money, and she commissioned him to make a birdbath in the shape of a fish.

Fierce bluejays fought outside her window every morning over breakfast crumbs. Perhaps she thought that a civilized birdbath would make them behave, or perhaps it would give her a root, a hold on the mountainside. How many times had she been uprooted, following her restless husband around the world?

She paid Bobby enough to buy a train ticket east, where he had taken a job on the crew of a sailing ship. Sailboats were my only rivals then. Without his distracting presence, I would be able to pay more attention to Maria.

I realized that she worried about all of us and that her concerns gnawed at her thin frame. Totally dedicated to her husband's career, she had no secret area of her own, no selfish pleasure to retreat to; all her energies went into the management of her family.

It was easier to relax with Rose, to laugh at money, to simply let life happen, even if there were stomach cramps each time the gray Chevrolet appeared on the horizon.

My grandmother was a strange mixture of Old World grande dame and intellectual adventuress. As the former, she was used to being financially provided for by "the system"—her middle-class parents' capital, my grandfather's failing business. It had floated her through life until now. With one foot still in the nineteenth century, she grew up in a world where men took care of women. Now here she was, dependent on Aldous. She venerated him as a genius and apparently simply took him for granted as a provider. Our presence did not appear to concern her much. She went about her daily routines totally absorbed by the delightful Olivia.

I watched the matronly old lady dress herself through a half-opened door one morning and was puzzled by the distance between us. Perhaps she locked herself away in her growing deafness. Once, like a malevolent witch, she took my upper lip between two fingers and predicted, "Some day this will be quite hairy."

Bonne Maman kept up a lively correspondence with Henry Miller, that expert on the art of borrowing. I was present one day when Aldous opened a telegram from him that read simply, "Please send five hundred dollars immediately." Disconcerted, Aldous asked Maria, "Should I send it, darling?" And she, immediately on the defensive, assured him, "No reason at all, sweetens." Maria was defending the rights of her own family, which did not include her mother's correspondents. She had wished us all safe. Now that we were here in her charge, it was time we learned the American work ethic.

Aware of the situation, I took action. Our own travel money was coming to an end, so I began to peruse the newspapers. There were jobs of all kinds available in Los Angeles. We moved to the city where the Huxleys kept an

odd furnished apartment like a hotel suite, with uphol-
stered armchairs complete with antimacassars. The only
personal, tempting place to sit was a sofa covered with an
Indian blanket to which a note had been pinned: "Please
don't sit on my bed. Signed, Matthew." This mysterious
cousin, Aldous and Maria's only son, whose bed was so hard
to avoid, remained absent. He was doing his medical studies at the time.

As a Smith College graduate, I was hired in an elegant
bookstore in Hollywood. For my sister, I found a job as an
usherette in a movie house. We enjoyed our jobs, for we
were still "playing" at work. Aldous, too, was amused and
dropped in on me at the bookstore, a convenient excuse for
a walk. Too blind to drive, walking gave him independence
from Maria, his intrepid chauffeur. His walking habits
along the residential back streets of Hollywood, where he
was pursued by barking dogs, had caused him to be picked
up by the police as a vagrant. The deadly artificiality of
those streets did not seem to bother him. They were a stage
set through which he, with his languid body, wandered as
the only incongruously live character.

Maria read aloud to him all of *War and Peace* as well as a
story I had written. Her reports back to me were typical.
"Aldous says you'll be able to make a living with writing."
Conversations, even in his presence, often began like this:
"We think, don't we, Aldous?" or, "Isn't it true, sweetens,
that you said she writes well enough to earn money at it?"

Money, money, money. Her lesson sank into me. I had
reached the moment in life when I had to become financially independent. I had contributed money I had earned
translating a book from the French toward this holiday, but
holidays were coming to an end. Maria's frail, almost blind
husband could no longer be expected to help us as he had
during the war years. My own writing would be no excuse
for becoming a dependent rebel like Henry Miller. And so
I collected my twenty-five dollars a week from the book-

shop, while Sylvia, dressed in black satin pants and an apple-green jacket with braided shoulders, was picked up every night and escorted home after the show by Aldous. He watched over and guided his nieces with simple and touching solicitude. I shared his eye-training classes in the Bates System and we exercised side by side. With an evident penchant for Sylvia's well-rounded figure, he said to his wife, "She reminds me of you, Maria, when I first met you. And you know, I think I'd marry you again."

On weekends we all lunched together at the Farmer's Market, where we met the Huxleys' friends Salka Viertel, Iris Tree, and her son Ivan Moffat. It was here that Sylvia and I introduced Aldous to Igor Stravinsky, who was eating his chicken a few tables away. We had met him the night before at a party. A Lucullan feast was planned; Vera Stravinsky made piroshki, Bonne Maman made a *pièce montée,* Uncle Billy roasted a lamb. The Stravinskys came to a family luncheon in the desert. From then on Aldous and Igor were fast friends.

Encouraged by Aldous, I wrote an article about Stravinsky. He also arranged for me to meet his friend Christopher Isherwood, who, with boyish good nature, became a willing subject for my beginner's journalistic efforts at writing a profile.

Aldous also allowed me to interview him for an article I was asked to write for *Vogue,* and again we walked together as I put to him impossible questions about Life and the Future of the World. Tolerant, he corrected my hasty assumptions, but his views of the world were persistently catastrophic.

Yet the war was ended, my studies were over, and I was in love. I refused to be impressed.

I was, in fact, resisting a certain psychic power, a mental witchcraft practiced here in California. Miracle diets, Eastern religions, and fortune-tellers were taken seriously. Aldous's latest hobby was to classify everyone into the three human types devised by William Sheldon. While explaining about endomorphs, ectomorphs, and mesomorphs, he suddenly turned to me with a wicked grin. In those days, I was an obvious long-and-thin ectomorph, as he was. "I think you're actually a P.P.S.," he said, meaning a Picnic Package Surprise. I now saw myself growing heavily mustached and hugely fat in middle age, thanks to his and Bonne Maman's predictions. This was unacceptable, and I fought my way with stubborn contrariness out of this spider's web.

One day a letter arrived from an editor at Simon & Schuster. Having read my first published story in *Junior Bazaar,* this editor wrote, "If ever you should be writing a novel let us know." Another such letter arrived a week later from an equally respectable publisher, enough to turn a young girl's head.

My future now seemed secure, and my return to New York essential. What this as yet nonexistent novel would be about, I had no idea. But New York was the place to be, and I was wanted there. I promptly left my job, as did Sylvia. My mother's exhibition, attended by Charlie Chaplin, Stravinsky, and Greta Garbo, had been a success. She had sold several pieces. And so we drove east again, leaving Maria, a small woman standing by the roadside. She waved at us with all the worries of the world in those eyes that were usually pale as water but that today were cloudy with anxious fretting. Just as Aldous worried about the fate of the universe, so she worried about each member of her family, and I knew that she would keep us in her mind till we were safely back on the other coast.

No doubt their concerns consumed them. They were the first to die, to leave our scattered tribe, while we lived on in this foolish, brave new world. My novel, of course, would not materialize for years. I got married instead and had four children. "Too many. Shame on you!" Aldous scolded when the fourth was born.

A few days after Aldous's death, his face looked up at me from *Newsweek* magazine. I was lying on my bed, back home on Long Island, the easternmost tip of the continent. For an instant he was so vividly present in that room, with an eerie, ironic smile, his elegant right hand lifted as if to communicate some final message, that I grew scared. I had always suspected him of being a kind of wizard. I knew of his healing hands, his experiments with E.S.P., his friendship with mediums, his fascination with drugs. Now the room was filled with laughter. The curled-up camel's lip, the beautiful blind eyes, the wave of the hand all seemed to make light of me, the foolish niece who still clung to the earth.

I shook him off, and the presence left the room. Better not, I thought. They have no right, up there, in their disembodied sphere, to laugh at our unfinished experiment.

15
MARRIAGE

There was a time when it seemed to be going out of fashion, the wedding as a milestone in one's life. During the sixties and seventies, people slipped in and out of cohabitation with the least possible ceremony. As I sat waiting for my children to make a definite commitment, I found myself dreaming with nostalgia about a vast festivity in white, white on green lawns, a gathering of clans, a reassurance that things will go on. Clearly, weddings were invented for and by parents, the witnesses. The couple in question is merely a sacrificial offering on the altar of tradition.

The further back I go, the more evident this seems. My Bonne Maman's wedding pictures are profoundly sad. There she sits in huge ballooning white sleeves, her hands folded in her lap, flanked by two aged matrons who wear yards and yards of black silk, ribbons, *passementerie*, braids, lace, sequins, silk flowers, brooches, and bonnets, and whose black high-button shoes stick out from beneath all this looking hot and vicious. The husband, poor innocent Bon Papa, does not even sit next to her but is also flanked by two convex-busted female guardians. He has a small, pointed beard and a silly curled mustache; his hands are white-gloved and his arms are crossed as if in determination to go through with the grim business that is expected of him. The other men stand in the back, peeking roguishly from behind walrus mustaches over the frizzy heads of the festooned females.

It was a *mariage de convenance*. Bonne Maman was in love with Bon Papa's brother and married Bon Papa as a second best. I can't help thinking that between these two Flemish dry goods families, the one dealing in linen and lace and the other in wool, there must have been a solid business arrangement and that the marriage of their children was just another occasion to display the wares in which they dealt.

By the time my mother married, thank God, the yardage required had diminished considerably. She looks unencumbered in a straight white gown loosely draped over the hip, though her neck is encircled by a choker. She wears pointed white shoes decorated with flowerlets. Attention has been paid to details and money spent to "do things right." Father seems to be enjoying the affair; he is a man who has caught his beautiful butterfly, as he addressed her in his love letters. Yes, they look liberated and slightly ironic. My mother, after all, was a free woman who had lived with the Huxleys in a witty, modern world in England and had been exposed to all the latest ideas. Embarrassed by the white spats Father wore when he came to ask for her hand, she later dressed him entirely in more artistic corduroy. Why do all these costumes seem important? Are clothes more representative of our real selves than we think? The bouquet consists of lilies of the valley and the long veil is made of delicate Flemish lace.

This veil was one of the prize possessions we brought over when emigrating to America but, significantly, I first wore it in a theatrical production at Smith, when I acted the bride in a French farce written at the time of my grandmother's wedding. The subject of the play was money, of course, a dowry. Possibly weddings are meaningless without dowries and daughters without "portions" doomed to mere concubinage.

Yet I also wore the veil, spotted indelibly with greasepaint, at my own wedding to Bobby, the suitor, though my dowry consisted of no more than a bed, some velvet curtains, and eight hundred dollars I had earned writing articles for *Vogue*. I had the strange illusion that I was a career woman and would earn my own living, which I considered a much more honorable form of dowry.

Clearly, our wedding was not a practical one. We were dreamers. A poet and a sculptor have no business setting up house, but the house and studio were given to us and everyone seemed so pleased with it all. The war had just ended and there had been so much dying that we were all in a hurry to start living again. At any rate, there is another wedding picture to study, my own. We all look a bit surprised that it has happened in this hurried, higgledy-piggledy fashion — on the unmowed lawns of the house my parents had recently bought in Islip, Long Island, in borrowed clothes, on the hottest day of the year.

Though my first visit to the Whites' great house in St. James had been like a prophetic dream, the next one had been somewhat traumatic. When Bobby brought me home to spend the weekend, he was received at the door by his mother, who handed him a tuxedo and a white shirt. He was then rushed off to a ball in Westbury, his last chance at a fortune, for the girl of the day was a Whitney. These social conventions were as baffling as the ones at Smith College, and I was too bewildered to be offended. Obviously, to belong in the Social Register required more than a line of banter.

I spent that evening with Bobby's many brothers and sisters, who adopted me as one of their own and whose conversation was delightfully original. Upstairs in the big house, the rooms were icy cold. We huddled together wrapped in scarves and listened to records of Stravinsky and jazz, after which one of the girls told me I could marry her brother if I wished. She had already promised him to various other friends, which later caused me some embarrassment, but her generosity was touching. When Bobby returned, he announced that he preferred to dance with me and that he did not feel at home in society. For one thing, he could not bear to wear shoes.

From then on his sisters began expecting us to elope. Alida even bought us a present, an antique door knocker, thinking that perhaps we were married already, and yet no formal announcements were made. It was all hopelessly vague, as life becomes when one is hanging around barefoot, neither in school nor properly married. Art, of course, was our excuse. Bobby sculpted and I was writing, having turned down a perfectly good job to devote myself to a major creative effort that never quite materialized, and to reading Carson McCullers, Truman Capote, and Jean Stafford, whom I tried to emulate.

So we hung around together for a year, traveling back and forth across Long Island between Islip and St. James. Our fathers played billiards together at the Century Club and our mothers arranged formal dinner parties *en famille*, hoping something would come of it, some definite announcement, some declaration of intent, some commitment. But at the appropriate moment for making meaningful toasts, our fathers always began telling jokes and evading the subject of matrimony. Bobby continued receiving invitations to debutante balls in New York and proceeded to bring me along, much to the astonishment of the hostesses. Unused to the milieu, I wore a faded blue gown, a hand-me-down from one of my mother's friends, and a black Spanish scarf with long fringes, exotic garb among the girlish fineries of the debutantes.

When we finally decided that summer to do it formally — "for my mother's sake," as Bobby put it — everyone seemed surprised. "You can't support her," said Father. "Besides, I have no money in the bank." But we prevailed, and I lent Father the first money I had earned with my writing to buy the champagne.

The newspapers called to ask what we would wear. Astonished, I heard my resourceful sister improvise on the telephone. It sounded just right, just like what one of those debutantes would wear if she had managed to catch my Bobby.

And here it all is in the photograph, an odd assortment, not at all what you'd expect from the newspaper's description. What are we doing there, standing in a row, looking so hot and solemn? The men are dashing but rather old-fashioned in their prewar finery — Father in a cutaway coat a little stretched across his stomach, my father-in-law in a splendid white starched waistcoat with a pair of clippers in his coat pocket that he would use throughout the wedding lunch to clip the shrubbery. Bobby wears his debutante party suit, the last time he would need it. But whatever is my mother doing in long black mittens and one of those squashed hats, and Sylvia in an evening gown from the thirties with padded shoulders and a draped bosom? Obviously, once again the box of hand-me-downs had provided the last-minute attire. I am wearing my sister-in-law's wedding dress, taken in here and there, and look quite elegant, except for a certain tragic expression. Had I been crying, was I another one of those sacrifices to tradition, or had I been bitten by mosquitoes?

I remember the eve of my wedding, an eerie hot and still August night during which no one slept, least of all me.

Waiting in vain for my beauty sleep, I first heard Mother prowling around restlessly, on tiptoe, oh, so quietly. When she finally retired to her room, I began to roam myself.

Downstairs all was unnaturally tidy in the high Victorian rooms of this house in Islip, which did not fit us yet—as if it, too, had been borrowed—decorated with white jasmine and tuberoses, maddeningly sweet. Tables were covered with monogrammed white cloths dating back to Mother's family in St. Truiden. Empty platters and polished silver shimmered in the moonlight. Everything was white, even the garden, where I wandered to see what sunflowers do at night when there is no sun to turn to. I had seeded them myself, thinking of Dutch gardens, but this house was tall and dwarfed them, and tonight their heavy heads simply drooped. An owl hooted hoarsely as if it had asthma, and all those lighted bedroom windows were reflected in hot, yellow pools on the untidy lawns. My mother's—was she mending our socks, as she had done during the difficult war years to calm her nerves? Father's—he was no doubt still trying to read volume one of Motley's *Rise of the Dutch Republic*, his head wrapped in a pale blue shawl, his bedside table covered with the large variety of pills with which he exorcised the tensions of middle age. Now I heard him curse at mosquitoes and slap naked flesh. They had moved into the house during the winter, and not yet realized the necessity of more adequate screens in the semitropical damp heat of Long Island.

Sylvia turned on her lights then, too. Now they were all keeping the vigil, yet it was three o'clock in the morning and each one was pretending to rest unperturbed on the eve of this festive occasion.

White—so cold, so pure—it obsessed me that night. Did not nuns dress in white when they chose Christ as their spouse? Bompa, lying motionless and dead, his hands folded, in the little parlor of our ancestral home, had been dressed in a white pleated nightgown. When I returned to my room and saw the satin dress hanging in the moonlight, I burst into tears. Yesterday we were children, Sylvia and I; tomorrow I would assume this white habit, this solemn wedding garment, and undertake a commitment to last "until death do us part." The funereal smell of the tuberoses seeped into the room and, lying once more on my bed, I imagined myself at my own burial.

It was then, in the first bleak light of dawn, that I had a visitation out of my past: my first teacher and guardian, Mr. Pimput, the imaginary companion of my childhood. A more ridiculous, pitiful creature would have been hard to find, for his narrow body had shrunk while mine had grown to adulthood. His white, transparent face trembled at the suggestion of light or sound. His pale, opaque eyes looked preoccupied, and I knew he saw not only me but the whole world at once, as well as other worlds whose existence I was unaware of. His hands, long and narrow, moved about busily yet with awkward clumsiness. He sat in front of an empty loom, lifting slender tuning forks to his ear and listening intently. He was too absorbed in this occupation to acknowledge my presence.

"What are you doing here on the eve of my wedding?" I asked him, resenting the way he ignored me after all these years of neglect.

"I am making words," he said in a whisper, his head bent to one side. My Mr. Pimput had a way of becoming people who had meant much to me: first he resembled Uncle Eric, the poet, and now those blind, all-seeing eyes were like those of both my favorite English teacher at college, Mr. Robert Gorham Davis, and Uncle Aldous. All these men had been wordsmiths and had attempted to teach me their craft. "I not only make words but the words call to me and I liberate them. Words hate to be unspoken," he explained. "You see, my loom is like a radio station. The words report here when they are anxious to be born and I emit them in all languages."

"But I hear nothing," I said, puzzled.

"Oh, no! No, no!" He shook his birdlike head. "I do not make *sound* but *existence.*" He held the tuning fork to his ear and passed his hand through the empty loom. "The air is so full of words," he sighed.

I was annoyed with him at first for being preoccupied with such abstractions, expecting some more concrete and meaningful advice. Then I distinctly saw two loaves of Italian bread I had bought that morning, the one round and the other long. Their crusts were brown, they smelled fresh, they were crisp and delicious. Mr. Pimput's voice said loudly, "This is the sign, the round loaf and the long one."

Marriage, I concluded as I awoke from the dream, grateful to the messenger of the night, was a kind of embodiment of abstractions, the word made flesh, mind and matter combined, and I forgot my funereal fears. White dresses, rings, ceremonies were words, concepts made visible. Why not?

Now the most concrete results of married life, my children, are hanging about somewhere, going their own ways, each with his own pursuit: physics, dancing, painting. I long to tell them that Mr. Pimput's cryptic message has pinned me down to earth, which is not such a bad place to be.

16
HOUSES

When my children were small, I was still a child myself. They clung to me like barnacles and cuffed at each other the way animals do, so that I had to constantly tear them apart.

The oldest was a prize, beautiful as a cherub, curly and frivolous. "What a social butterfly!" said Bobby's Great-Aunt Luisa approvingly when he was only three. Later she chose him as her Casino partner and taught him how to cheat. But that was when he was seven and had lived "abroad," which gave him an added glamor in Aunt Luisa's eyes.

The second was plain and fierce and lay frowning in a ball on my bed like a porcupine. This delighted me. Every time I looked at her I burst into surprised laughter. Her brother at first resented her presence and attacked her wholeheartedly.

"No," I protested. "Get away." I wanted my porcupine to be a secret I kept from the world until it stopped frowning.

The farmer's wife next door put up eggs in water glass. They cost nothing but tasted peculiar. The milk of our goat smelled dreadful. We lived on a monthly check of one hundred dollars from the G.I. bill and so living off the land was a necessity. I dug for clams and picked beach plums and made bread to sell to various neighbors, filling my baby carriage with loaves as well as babies. We lived on air and were messy and careless. When the days grew long, we trekked into the woods or along the shore. I fell in love with tree men dressed in orange. The fields were full of crows, huge black things flopping about.

But after five years of this earthbound, domestic life, I began to long for something to happen, something besides babies. The farmhouse in which we lived was like an incubator, lying brooding and still through long winter snows. I was growing restless and bored with the view on a potato field to the south, the row of arborvitae to the west. Staring at these dark trees through my window, I had decided that they too felt trapped, rooted there around the lawn, and giving them names, I let them run away at night through the moonlight. Hop, Isebrilde! Off with you, Pantalion! And along gardens and hedges they would glide in my mind, but every morning when I woke up they were dutifully back in place, standing guard, like me, over this plot of Long Island ground.

I could walk in various directions, pushing my well-filled carriage, and have tea in the grand old houses belonging to in-laws that dotted the landscape. They had been planned originally as summer residences but were now inhabited year round by lonely survivors of a past era. Charley Butler, a hugely round gentleman farmer, would pour thick cream into my tea and waltz me around on surprisingly dainty, nimble feet. His neighbor, Cousin Suzy Huntington, had deliciously fine china but suffered from a strange propensity for weeping, so that suddenly, in the middle of tea, tears poured down her cheeks. This was disconcerting and made conversation difficult. Her children had married and left her, and her house had grown too large, just as her skin had grown loose on her body. Large houses needed to justify their existence by being full of children, I decided; otherwise, they became melancholy.

In that sense, Aunt Alida Emmet's house was justified, but at the price of a perpetually prolonged childhood for its inhabitants. Her teas were delicious, her summonses tyrannical but irresistible. Her house, like a ship sailing out into the sky, stood on top of a bluff overlooking the sound. On winter afternoons, I sat in her parlor and watched the red sun sink down into the frozen sea until the Irish maid came and drew the curtains and brought in the hot biscuits.

Listening to timid footsteps in the halls above, I wondered each time, "What are they *doing!*" For this was a house full of living ghosts. They trailed down from upstairs rooms, wispy and tall, with hankies tucked into the sleeves of their sweaters. "Just a little sniffle," Jane said faintly. She was the youngest of Aunt Alida's middle-aged children, an old girl with bobbed gray hair and a thin neck. Her older sister, Margaret, was deaf but more robust. "Cunning," she smiled at my son. "Isn't he cunning!" My porcupine they examined doubtfully. "They often change you know. Plain babies often turn into perfect beauties."

"She has a lot of character," I protested defensively.

Beauty was important here. Life-size portraits of Jane and her sister hung in the living room, two young girls wearing low-waisted sleeveless satin dresses with deep décolletage. A third sister had died in full flower and therefore remained the most beautiful of all.

My children stuffed on biscuits and ran around the rooms screaming. Sometimes Willy came down, unshaven and distinctly odd. "Perfectly delightful," he would say, sidling up to the cakes, which he crumbled absent-mindedly into his pocket. The palms of his hands were as red as a monkey's. "It's so boorring here," he sighed. "In England

the garden parties were so delightful, everyone in white on
the lawns, don't you know." The assumption that I knew was
flattering. "Eurrup is so delightful." They all rolled their *r*s
in the back of the throat. "French *r*s," they explained. They
had chosen me as their teatime entertainment because,
being a "foreigner," I would understand their predilection
for Eurrup.

"Is Mother coming down?" asked Jane anxiously. "She
hasn't been too well." And indeed, Aunt Alida, a Catholic
convert, most often lay in bed with her rosaries — several of
them draped over the four bedposts, one in her hand — as if
the more rosaries, the more effective the prayer. There did
not seem to be anything specially wrong with her, but she
believed in saving up her energies. "You last longer that
way," she had told me with a wink, and had summoned me
to entertain her children. But what excitement could I
possibly provide for these idle ghosts? Perhaps it was the
sight of my babies she thought would be beneficial. Was it
her doing, I wondered, this perpetual dependence of
theirs?

"I could have been an opera singer if my legs hadn't been
so long," sighed Willy. "Nowadays they can fix that, cut a
piece out of the legs to make them shorter." No one
laughed at this, but it was clearly too late now to attempt a
career. Jane and her deaf sister played the recorder
together for me, a tune they had composed, but the harmony was a bit off and their playing breathy. "Lovely!" I
said, glad they had tried. Then they quarreled because Jane
didn't count "one . . . two . . . three . . ." before starting.
My little boy, meanwhile, had wandered off to the kitchen,
where the Irish cook and the parlor maid danced the jig
for him.

At last Tommy came down and the conversation picked
up. Tommy, being a gossip, was the only one who would tell
me about "the past," when his brother and sisters were
pursued throughout Europe by dukes and duchesses. This

made the ladies disappear instantly, each wiping away a tear with her hanky. Willy had already drifted into the library, where he wore a green eyeshade and read movie magazines.

"I think she'll have a Eurruppean nose," Tommy remarked, trying to be pleasant about the porcupine who sat on my lap, staring at him fiercely.

"You were talking about Davos," I reminded him.

"Oh, yes. We spent much time there, since Jane's lungs were supposed to be bad. I was only a child then. It was so annoying, for Margaret was always falling in love. I could tell at once by the way she flushed, and then she'd make me deliver letters to a young man who wore spats and called me *Bübchen*. Sometimes I threw the letters down the laundry chute."

"What happened to the gentleman?"

"Oh, he died. One day you'd hear them cough and the next day they'd be wheeled off, dead."

"Goodness!"

Tommy's favorite sister had been Libba, the beauty, whose portrait hung over the mantle. "When we entered a room, everyone stared." He was living on that past glory, entering rooms with Libba. He still tried it on his own now and then, entering one shoulder at a time, looking about with a proud challenge, flaring his nostrils, but without Libba the effect was not the same.

"Jane was very passionate, you know. She ran off once with a black jazz musician, but I brought her home, poor thing. He had stolen her pearls."

"Home? Where was home? Here, on Long Island?"

"Goodness, no. Until the war began to threaten, we led a nomadic existence for as long as I can remember. Hotels, on the whole. We lived in hotels, in London or Switzerland. Mummy and Daddy used to go hunting in Ireland a lot, but we preferred society in the city."

Finally Aunt Alida came down, dressed in a black velvet robe trimmed with fur, and called out, "Where is everyone? We're having a party, a nice party." And loudly she summoned all her children to attend. "And you," she challenged me with piercing eyes. "Have you done your Easter duty yet?"

Aunt Alida's attempts to monitor my soul struck me as horribly indiscreet. I felt my face blush bright red. "Aha!" she cried. "I've got you there!" Hurriedly I tried to gather my children, buttoning the porcupine's coat to escape her tyrannical presence. "Come, we're leaving!"

But my little boy escaped, seized Aunt Alida's cane, and began to ride it around the room as if it were a hobbyhorse. "Aunt Alida is a witch, Aunt Alida is a witch," he sang. She laughed loudly at this. Her favorite could do no wrong, but having noticed my confusion, she would not let me be. "You're just upset because you're pregnant, my dear, perfectly natural!" Furious, I wondered how she could see inside my womb as well as my soul. These last three months I had been trying to hide this impractical pregnancy of mine, for we were about to leave on a journey.

I grabbed the children and muttered, "She really is a witch," as I drove off with them through the cabbage fields, tears rolling down my cheeks. No wonder her children were reduced to shadows, living on their memories of Eurrupp and Society, in perpetual banishment like White Russian émigrés. It struck me as ironic that here on Long Island, where I was living a supposedly American life, I should, as my only entertainment, be listening to these French *r*s, these tales of a past belonging to a vanished world.

In summer, postcards began to arrive from Europe. To console Sylvia after an unhappy love affair, Mother could think of nothing better than to send her to Florence. Pictures of the Duomo, however, did not make me jealous.

"Eurrupp," I scoffed. "Who needs it? All that culture, it's all in the past. It's just for tourists."

My children were American and spoke its idiom. "Our Father, Who art in heaven, Hollywood be Thy name," my son recited dutifully. And yet I longed to travel, but realized that, being pregnant once more, this would be impractical. So I had kept my secret hidden from everyone, only to be exposed by Aunt Alida.

"Perhaps you could get a job teaching out in Wyoming or South Dakota," I suggested to Bobby. Long Island was, after all, only a tiny part of the United States, an arm reaching out toward Europe. But Bobby would hear none of it. Instead, he won a fellowship at the academy in Rome. I had married a man of talent!

During our move to Rome, the barnacles clung to me for dear life. I now became the ground to them — their country, their house, their everything. What had we done, uprooting them so early? Not only the first two, but also this third one swimming inside me. In my dreams, I lost them. They climbed out of portholes, got left behind in trains, ran away through strange city streets. We tied them to us with ropes day and night. "Eurrupp," I thought, "is a place to get lost in. It's no longer home." And I longed for tea in the safe, cozy parlor of Aunt Alida's house on the bluff, an ark braving the sea of time.

For three years we lived in makeshift fashion, first in an ugly rented basement apartment, then in an unheated penthouse, all five in one bed in the stable of a Florentine village, then in a pensione where we ate daily broth with noodles, then in two cramped rooms hanging onto a rock in Ravello on the Amalfi coast, and, the last summer, in a Dutch farmhouse that smelled of pig. The two oldest children began to speak a multilingual gibberish. They picked up diseases: jaundice, whooping cough, chicken pox, dysentery, pneumonia. Bravely they made friends, only to leave them behind at every move. I took them out for daily

airings in Roman parks among the statues and fountains
and peacocks, where they observed immaculately dressed
children called Julio Cesare and Marc Antonio, but they
soon tired of these well-behaved outings and preferred to
play in the street with gangs of ragamuffins. Their vocabu-
lary of swear words became tremendous.

"It's time we went home," I told Bobby, home meaning
America, Long Island, the house with the faithful trees
standing guard, as well as all those relatives, those
matriarchs and bachelor cousins, that whole landscape of
coziness and continuity.

But before we returned I took them to see my childhood
houses, going first to the one in Roermond, on the small
side street sliding down toward the city ramparts. We
turned the corner and there it was, with its four steps
climbing to the front stoop, the leaded panes in the tall
windows. But the cement facade was a dirty gray in the
rain. Could it ever have seemed elegant and enormous?
"This is it," I said. Perhaps my Proustian immersion in
memories of the past are irksome to Bobby, for his reaction
was puzzling.

"Oh," he said, and checking whether anyone was coming
from left or right, he peed against the wall of the house. It
was a strange gesture of defilement.

"Why did you do that?" I asked, offended.

"I don't know," he shrugged. "The house has nothing to
do with you anymore."

We then went up north and I took them to the house by
the sea, still owned by my parents but inhabited all through
the war by a painter and his wife. They had not paid their
rent all these years, but to my delight the roof was freshly
thatched, the little gate had been painted, and the roses
bloomed in the garden. With a pounding heart, I walked
up the path to the kitchen door. A friendly middle-aged
woman opened it. "I am Claire Nicolas and I was born in
this house. Do you mind if I show it to my family?" She

stared at me with surprised terror and, no doubt thinking I had come to claim possession, burst into tears and sobbed, "I had forgotten that it doesn't belong to me."

So much for houses. We shed them like snakes their skins, but as long as we inhabit them they are our nests, from which new lives are launched, they are our very bodies, containing generations of memories. Inside them we hear time's echo, the way the sea echoes through the empty chambers of a shell.

17
CIRCLES

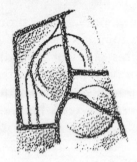

If my parents had not returned to live in Holland, in that provincial backwater of Limburg, I would have left it at that—a glimpse of houses no longer mine, the realization that memories are, after all, not to be revisited. I might have severed the umbilical chord.

But they were clever at rebuilding new homes. They got better and better at it, and when Father was lured back in 1958 by the greatest commissions of his life, he gave up the difficult struggle to become American with little regret.

And so here it is, a four-hundred-year-old farmhouse with a tile roof in the middle of the meadows near the river. All the treasures are here: Emérence's china from St. Truiden, Bompa's fragments of stained glass, antique cabinets restored by Uncle Charles, ancient oak tables, and the paintings and sculptures made before, during, and after the war, transported across oceans and looking perfectly at home.

By 1963 there are bedrooms here for my children, studios for all of us, a garden filled with fruit—cherries, wild strawberries, apples, raspberries—and shelves upon shelves of jams and preserves made by Mother for "when you come!"

So, of course we go, but at first only on the way to visit friends in France and England. Later, I come alone.

It is quite pointless, my still clinging to a picture of Father as an arrogant, vain, sensuously handsome man of forty, for I have come to verify the fact that he is old and insists, with all his gifts for melodrama and self-pity, on being old. His smooth bald head, from which the features droop in heavy pockets, is like a caricature of old age. Even Mother, with her little girl's haircut and astonished eyes, her elegant, thin-lipped mouth, her quivering, ninety-pound figure, is caught in a net of wrinkles, like a butterfly fluttering in a spider's web.

How could this have happened to them? Indignant at their transformation, I lie in a bed too small for me at 9:30 in the evening and feel myself nodding off against my will, once more overcome by the passivity of childhood.

Upstairs in his "nest," a bed rarely made, he lies with his nightcap on, reading *Paris-Match* for the fourth consecutive evening. Tomorrow he will switch to *Newsweek*, over which she has been brooding for the last three days. A brief conversation will occur at breakfast about their mutual findings. There are books by his bedside, mostly Latin and Greek classics, which he knows by heart. These companions comfort him. He explains with anatomical glee that since his last attack, probably a slight stroke, he has been suffering a brain disease with an unpronounceable name that makes it hard for him to read. But his brain functions brilliantly if he wants it to, and his disease is mostly impatience with contemporary trends in art and literature that have passed him by. And so he rechews the classics, "which those ignorant fellows never bothered to read," and presently falls asleep, only to wake up toward three A.M. I, too, wake up then to hear him pace the floor and rummage among his medicines for an appropriate pill.

On the other side of my bedroom wall, Mother lies in the bed in which I was born. For half an hour I hear her fluttering and tossing like a fish out of water. Her energetic body does not relax, is unable to lie still, until the magic of the sleeping pill has got its hold on her and she sinks, motionless, into deep slumber.

At nine in the morning, their shrunken bodies loosely draped in bathrobes, they shuffle about and report on the battle of the night: tales of indigestion, insomnia, neuralgia, worries, and nightmares. But whereas her energies build up to a crescendo that reaches its peak in the early afternoon, he has by then returned to his room to dive back into sleep, to apocalyptic visions and forebodings of death.

"But he has always done that!" my sister reassures me. "Ever since Bompa died he has frightened us with these morbid predictions, don't you remember?"

Why is it that everyone else sees through these threats of his while I fall for them again each time, as I did that night in New York when he announced his intention to commit suicide and rushed out of the house? Then I worried and wept, while my mother and Sylvia were not the least surprised at seeing him return an hour later with the newspaper. Now I still tremble for him, even as I consider his threats an unfair technique for arousing my sympathies. A cup of coffee seems to be all it takes to return him from the grave.

"There's nothing wrong with you," I say. "You're just trying to scare me!" He looks hurt, defensive. But Mother, the professional spouse, cocks her bird's head, pats his knee, and humors him sweetly. "Not at all! He feels terrible. I do feel sorry for you, darling." He lowers his eyes, accepting the soothing words as his due. She knows that the truth is less real than the ceremonies we perform for one another, the inventions that make life bearable. With her concessions she has gained the upper hand and can now take her revenge by leading him by the nose.

"Go on, eat your apple!" she says, taking a wormy one out of her gardening basket and putting it on his plate.

"But I don't want an apple."

"Don't be a fool. It's good for you." There's no disobeying her. We must all eat her apples. If necessary she'll peel them, cut out the worms, and shove them into our mouths herself. A perpetual mother, though half our size, hers is a tyranny of devotion. She buttons his shirt and cuts his meat as if he were senile, tells me to blow my nose and not to eat with my fingers.

I have just been to visit her sister Jeanne, now remarried to a whimsical poet whom she locks in his studio all day to work. This time she is determined to hold onto her man and claims to be an expert. She has grown domestic, plump.

"Your mother is possessed," she told me. "She is unreasonable and possessed. I have given up on her."

"Possessed by what?" I asked. Her sad brown eyes and sensuous mouth were knowing.

"By willpower," she said. I realized that sibling rivalry was still at work here, that this woman of experience had since childhood tried to put down Mother and to keep her in her place. But Mother finally is no longer dominated by anyone; she dominates. The "stupid one"—as Jeanne used to call her unfairly—no longer keeps quiet, but asserts her opinionated self all over the place. My tyrannical father has become the victim and, reluctantly, I admit that it is only fair, justice has been done. And yet, unreasonable myself, I feel the need to protest, to state my independence.

"I don't have to blow my nose. Stop bossing me!"

The perfectly round eyes open wide. She is deeply hurt.

"It's only for your own good," she says. She picks up her apple basket, pulls the empty coffee cups out of our hands, and busies herself loudly in the kitchen, moving hither and yon with the mindless agitation of a beetle against a windowpane.

This is the hour when, feeling chipper, he takes his walk. Though it is August, he puts on his bow tie, his gloves, his scarf, his coat, and picks up a hat and cane. We then inspect the neighborhood. The trees are his, the pigs, the brook, and if the neighbors' houses offend him, if their sewers smell or they have painted their woodwork the wrong color, he takes it as a personal insult. If, on the other hand, the wind makes the poplars wave and the moon appears over the river, he brags about it as if no one else owned such trees, such a moon.

On the way back, a neighbor is captured and brought home for a glass of sherry. Here again she has won, for the glass of sherry has replaced the vast array of stronger spirits with which, much to her disapproval, he used to inebriate his guests and himself. Now to my astonishment I hear him say to his guest in a disparaging tone of voice, "In America you have a luncheon appointment, you go to a club, you wait for your lunch and have a couple of Martinis. Those fellows drink like fish!" He likes to impress his friends by dwelling on his American experience. When I ask him to return for a visit he frowns, not the least bit tempted. The most difficult and frustrating period of his life has remained the adventure he could not master. Here in Limburg he is inextricably intertwined with the history, the landmarks, the grotesque dialect which I still cannot understand.

One rainy afternoon when we all feel trapped by the dismal weather, he decides to take me to see his grand-parents' house. In the pouring rain we drive through farm-land, a new suburb, and come upon the Tegelrij. It is a small manor house with a farmyard, a moat, solid and melancholy, the old brick walls darkened by rain. Seeing it, I remember the photograph of my Bomma as a girl, timid-looking in her Victorian trappings, prisoner of corset and stuffy silk. Her parents, wearing hats, sit in front of the Tegelrij on iron chairs at a round table while she is about to row around the moat in a rowboat. On the anniversaries of their deaths we used to go to Mass, after which Bomma served us a breakfast with hot rolls.

We sit and watch the house for a while through the rain. There is little to say. The ballroom on the first floor has remained as it was, he says. Did they really give balls in this dour province? I feel superior now, cosmopolitan and detached. I find Limburg oppressive, totally devoid of charm, and wonder how I could ever have called it home. Perhaps it is their country once more but it is no longer mine.

They are now traveling farther back, to the roots of things. Mother has been penning her memoirs. She shows me her voluminous scribblings. Apologetic, she adds, "You don't have to read it if it doesn't interest you." I am fascinated, but to my amazement these hundreds of pages cover only the first ten years of her life. I read about the games she played with her sisters, the dresses she wore, her mother, my Bonne Maman, weeping every morning at breakfast because she was unhappily married. Then we reach World War I, when the family became wanderers, cosmopolites, and the memoirs stop.

My mother puts on her woolen underwear and goes to the garden to dig potatoes. I watch her through the window furiously pulling and gathering. That little face will always seem ingenuous to me. Someone might still be tempted to sweep her off her feet, but I am also aware that she would only laugh at him. How sensible she has been, how self-effacing. At night she will creep hesitantly into my room to proffer affection, which I, a porcupine myself, shrug off. Then, unable to resist the temptation, she will sit on my bed and talk, but not as I imagine other mothers would. No, she refuses to behave as mothers are supposed to, and I, slightly embarrassed, am treated to the love affairs, real or imaginary, of her life.

"I often say to your father, goodness, how badly we behaved. Do you realize what we started? No wonder young people nowadays are confused, considering the example we gave them." Over and over she harks back to the story of Jeanne and her irascible lover, to the beautiful abandoned Nel, whom my father consoled a bit too tangibly, to the handsome poet, Adriaan Roland Holst, who remains the most romantic of her memories. How unimportant it all seems now, this scandal that people in Holland still whisper about at dinner parties, yet it was significant too, the way everything is that one remembers clearly, though perhaps incorrectly.

"Do you suppose that's why I've been such a puritan?" I ask her. It makes her laugh.

"You're like Bomma," she says. "Not like us at all."

Before we know it, it is three in the morning and we hear rumblings above. Father comes down to see what's stirring and, finding us at our gossip, looks a bit left out, as if he were jealous of our intimacy. Perhaps he guesses that some of the talk has been about the trials of a life spent at his side.

Poor Father. He was, after all, always outdone, for what man is stronger than a wife and two daughters? The odds are against him. And the more women he acquires, the larger grows the "other" camp. So Father remains there "above," in his upstairs room, the genius, the man, the tyrant, threatening at regular intervals to die and abandon us. It will be his final revenge.

18
HAPPINESS

Now it seems our house is haunted. "Impossible," I exclaim. "It's a happy house. All these windows, all these doors, a ghost could not hide here from the light." The young couple who house-sat while we were back in Europe report footsteps, noises, a presence that tore the coffeepot out of their hands repeatedly and threw it on the kitchen floor.

Two years ago an aging hippie with a long beard and a three-legged dog had reported the same symptoms, some force chasing him out of the house at night. We were surprised at first. This man was perhaps impressionable but not a coward. He had traveled all over the world on a motorcycle and had been chased by worse dangers than vague spirits, and so we laughed and forgot about it.

Now I'm beginning to wonder. Last night, waking in the dark after having slept in different rooms in different cities, different hotels, facing north, facing south, in mountains, in plains, I got up with a start and saw an oak cabinet carved by hand and Father's portrait of my mother as his fiancée. I saw white walls, wooden floors painted red . . . and wondered what charmed inn this could be, what rustic good taste had provided this comfort, these thick cotton sheets, this faint smell of woodsmoke and cleanliness. And suddenly I knew it was home and it seemed like heaven.

But to others it is haunted. Only we are tolerated here by someone who inhabits the house more faithfully, more possessively even, than ourselves. And so, to confirm these rumors, I visit my neighbor, a young woman of earthy beauty with a wide, generous mouth. Her children gather around her in her kitchen, asking for peanut butter, climbing on her lap, pulling her hair. She has only recently moved here and has no connection to our past history, but already her reputation as the granddaughter of a Cherokee witch, as a seer and medium of sorts in her own right, is spreading throughout the neighborhood.

"Yes," she says, "there is definitely a presence in your house. I always feel it. It is not sad, but is looking for something. I have never been upstairs, but is there a brown bureau with drawers? It is looking for something in the bureau."

I know who it is, of course, and am cross with it. This is no way to behave toward guests in the house, but how does one scold a ghost? Besides, it may be trying to tell me something, blaming me for my divided loyalties, my constant returning to that other world of the past.

We cohabit easily, we make room for each other and tolerate this shadow, this memory that is by now almost gay, playful. Though the piano is silent, it is hers. I sit writing at her desk, but her diary still lies in the bottom drawer, her red jacket hangs in the closet, the tapes of her voice singing *"Seben crudele, mi fai languir,"* are in the brown bureau. We never listen to them but they sing. Though it has been ten years now, people still avoid mentioning what happened, as if it were some shameful disease, as if the violence of an accident could wipe out seventeen years of happiness.

No doubt sad ghosts need airing, sweeping out, exorcising, chasing away, but one clings to the happy ones, in secret, savoring their presence with childish self-indulgence. Strangers cannot be expected to understand this. They are not prepared to have to share a space with what is not visible, and so collisions occur, coffeepots fly, and the ghost, irritated by their lack of awareness, begins to tease them with noises, to hide objects, and, grown tyrannical, to chase them out into the night.

"She always resented intruders," we tell ourselves with a tolerant smile. "She always guarded this house jealously." So we humor our ghost, nourish this fleeting spirit with our secret memories. It is not illogical that a life so suddenly, so violently interrupted should continue in our minds. Just as it is impossible to erase the past, so an interrupted life cannot be refused a future. I shall tell you the story of this daughter who died suddenly, in broad daylight, at the age of seventeen. But I shall tell it discreetly so as not to expose her, so as to keep her with us to watch over our house and our lives at the risk of some broken crockery, the sound of opening drawers, and footsteps in the attic when strangers are about.

First I must deal with the disappearance of the one who preceded her. I know that my sitting here, in this room filled with mementoes, writing about the past, is a form of exorcising, and so I shall go back to the reunion of Aunt Rose and my parents.

After twelve years of absence, Rose, twice widowed, has come from California where she still lives in the Mojave Desert, to visit my parents, who have come one last time to the United States. Here they sit around my dining room table in my house by the sea, midway between their final domiciles. Rose, the beauty, has grown fat. Her blue eyes, sung by Uncle Eric, the poet, are the only vestige of the magic that made men dream. Though the voice still trails off with delicious throaty overtones, still bubbles with laughter, her stories have become repetitious and one tends to lose the thread of them. Her wholesome appetites, her greedy mouth, all this is now lost in a melancholy of too much flesh—the flesh that once sang with Flemish joy in the nudes my father painted of her, floating arabesques of curves on a background of silver-gray pillows.

As she chatters away, Father, his eyelids heavy, listens and sometimes shakes his head as if her tale were not quite believable, while Mother, minute, trim as a bird, observes with superiority this younger sibling whose voice is an echo from the past. "But what are you talking about?" she says, and the story wanders on to Paris, to the World's Fair of 1937, then returns to a masked ball in Amsterdam in 1930, skips to a cabin in New Hampshire during the war, then mentions an Italian lover on a sailboat in the Zuider Zee.

"Ah," says my father as if he had suddenly penetrated a deep mystery. "You are talking about when *we* were still alive." He looks older than his years, his head bald and smooth, his expression ironic and detached.

It is autumn. The room has grown dark. It is like a ship too heavy with the weight of these three grown old. Perhaps I shall drown with them. Yet they are merry in their own way, merry with the lives, the stories that might have been passing dreams, of which only the telling is left. And I am merely the listener, the lifelong spectator. I, who once witnessed their adult world from a child's point of view, wondering whether someday I would move in such spheres of delight, ask myself where I have been in the interim. Have I been young and beautiful? What tale will I tell one day, twenty-five years from now, and will those who listen to me remember me as I am now and say, "It is true. That is the way it was"?

At this moment my youngest daughter, Natalie, enters the room and hands each of them a pink flower she has made out of wire and plastic, drawing us back into the present, away from the melancholy weight of past happiness.

Two years later I return to Holland while Father is working on what he calls his Last Window. I follow him up the steep stairs to the studio, and on the glass easel is the painting of the head of an old man lying on his deathbed, etched in black against the light. Two strange spotted dogs play by his bedside, their red tongues hanging out of their mouths. I think of Father's favorite saying: "From the sublime to the ridiculous takes only one step; I take the step in reverse." The dogs are grotesque in their lopsidedness but they are ennobled by the gravity of the dying king.

This window, which tells the story of the prophet Isaiah, will take several months to finish and be installed, and whenever he is at work on it he is totally immersed in its creation. When he is not, however, an annoying gloom seems to surround him. The death of a friend is mentioned and he keeps an ominous silence, sitting in the corner of the sofa, listening to our conversation as if he were already absent. He is acting out the tragic part of that king in his window, I think, and refuses to pay attention.

When the day comes for me to leave, he insists on taking me to the station and carries both my bags onto the train, playing father till the very end, still with the look of being the victim of some fatal joke. He is wide, solid, careful, but will not smile, and looks at me with the reproachful glance of one of those dogs in his window. This is intolerable, and tyrannically I order him to "be happy!" He shakes his head as if in protest. "Yes, yes, I'll be happy," he says, and leaves the train without looking back.

A few months later, the last window being installed, he is toppled by a heart attack just as he had always predicted, and I rush home once more for the funeral. We bury him in the grave he had reserved only two weeks before, at the foot of a Romanesque church on a hill overlooking the

meadows and river. A Gregorian choir sings and we admire
the windows he painted here: Saint Peter with his keys,
Saint Odilia with her eyes on a platter, Jonah regurgitated
by the whale.

Now I see him in some undefined locality where the
company is overwhelmingly aged, composed of all the
grandparents and great-uncles, all those predecessors
whose lives petered out before his. Then suddenly, three
years later, our youngest daughter, Natalie, joins him there,
distributing pink flowers to everyone.

To explain this unexpected event will not take long. It is a
very short story. Natalie was a young girl with wheat-
colored hair and a beauty spot over her upper lip (some
said it looked like chocolate, others like a bee bite). She
grew up in such a hurry to be perfect that we complained,
"She never sits in the parlor with us to chat," and her
friends asked, "Why don't you hang around by the railroad
station or in the candy store with us?" She would jump on
her bicycle and smile as if she knew a secret, saying, "I'm
busy," and ride off to our house, which stood alone in the
trees.

Afterward people used to say, "Do you remember how
transparent she was?" But it was not because she was frail.
God knows she had enough energy. It was rather as if she
were slightly incandescent, so that you felt like passing your
hand in front of your eyes to make sure she was really there.
This first became apparent when she was five and asked me
to take her out into the snow. We walked under the trees
and watched the tracks of small animals, the feathery
marks of their tails and their triple-toed imprints on the
whiteness. Blue shadows now appeared under her eyes and
she said solemnly, "My teacher told me to watch snow very
carefully, for it won't be there long."

At the age of nine she went to visit a friend on an island.
She was flown there in a plane, but no sooner did she land
than she began to cry with homesickness. She used up so

many boxes of tissue that her friend began to cry too. "It's not that I don't love you," she apologized. "It's that I'm wasting my time."

Time grew in the house where we lived. It lay about the rooms and in the attic, packed in trunks. It shone through the windows onto our beds. When the beds were empty she fretted, "When will we all be together again?" and she knitted ties of gray wool for her brothers, who were away in college, and sent them off in the mail. She filled the rooms with plants that climbed up the windows, and served tea with cookies almost anywhere. In one room she sewed real coats with linings and put in labels she had made with her name on them. The coats still hang in the closets. In the kitchen she baked birthday cakes and cooked Japanese dishes, frowning while chopping the zucchinis into slender strips. Sometimes she cleaned everything and sometimes nothing; sometimes she polished the silver on the Fourth of July. In another room she sang. This took several hours of time until, by late afternoon, after endless scales had been practiced, everything was ready for the voice. It rose in the twilight behind closed doors. It began childishly at first but already in many languages, and it grew to nearly that of a woman when it stopped. This is the voice that lies in tapes in a cigar box in her father's bureau drawer.

In the summer her sister, Stephanie, came home and then time dissolved into laughter. To entertain her she collected small kittens, a horse, and a dog like a unicorn. The dog lay most often upside down, showing his pink belly, between the four legs of the table. The horse she trained, braiding ribbons in its mane, and rode it wearing a cowboy hat.

Every winter day she got up at dawn without waking anyone and stood by the trees to wait for the schoolbus. She didn't miss a day, though I would say, "Why don't you stay home and sleep? Who cares about that stupid school?"

"I would miss my friends," she'd say. "They have problems, you know. Only I have no problems."

To buy material and thread with which to dress all of us, she scrubbed floors, minded stores and small children. These grew up to be as large as she, but many of them wondered why they were alive and waited for something to happen. She never waited. When music played she danced so hard, tossing her hair about, that young men wished she would stand still long enough for them to catch her. Not satisfied with being one person at a time, she acted the part of several on various stages, and old people who saw her said, "She is like a candle," and began to cry for no reason, remembering what they had forgotten to be. Since all the plays had happy endings, she finally decided to rest.

"Tomorrow," she said, "I shall go to the beach and get all brown so as to be ready." Ready for what?

But when she was ready, she disappeared. It happened instantly, on the way back from the beach, when a truck ran into her car. None of us realized at the time that this is what she had been working at with increasing intensity.

Sometimes she returns to me in dreams, to tidy the rooms I have messed up, and once she was almost tangible.

"Why did you come back?" I asked, reaching for the sweater she was wearing and on which I had seen her working night after night.

"Because I'm very sentimental," she said, but already the sweater began to unravel in my hands.

No doubt she is more visible in that place where my father dwells and where she will remain seventeen years old forever. I don't really grudge him her company, but we must at least be allowed our ghost. We have a right to it.

19
ARTIST'S
WIFE

Every now and then I need to be reminded that there is such a thing as genius. Being an artist's daughter, wife, and mother, I tend to become skeptical about this elusive quality. Perhaps it is merely a question of overwhelming energy. Whatever it is, every now and then one needs an encounter with the real thing to make life worth living.

As girls, Sylvia and I already considered talent a prerequisite in a future husband. I remember us walking home from the beach one day along Ocean Avenue, in the Long Island suburb where we lived briefly after the war. The beach was a scrappy one covered with flotsam and jetsam, the corpse of a sea gull eaten by worms, the paper-thin shells of horseshoe crabs. The water was muddy, gray, and shallow. Still, our skin had a pleasant salty taste and the house toward which we walked was a roomy Victorian one with large windows set in a fenced yard. We did not really feel at home in this sedate neighborhood. It did not fit our image of a suitable environment for avant-garde, artistic young women.

The war was over and, now of marriageable age, we were discussing our boyfriends. Being sisters, there was an inevitable tone of rivalry in our conversation.

"I think mine is a very good sculptor," I said ponderously. Thin and nearsighted, I moved with angular vagueness, as if floating through an intangible world. Bobby, my young man, had returned to art school after being discharged from the service, and had sent me photographs of his work. It had the impressionist surface of Epstein and the elongated forms of Lehmbruck. Both of these were sculptors whose statues I had admired in the Museum of Modern Art, and so I was favorably impressed. Even though I might be in love with him, I would never be able to share the life of a man whose work I did not respect.

My sister, a painter, was darker and moodier than I. Now, provoked by my approval of my fiancé's work, she said with a shrug that eliminated all competition, "The trouble is, he's a dilettante."

"If anyone is a dilettante, it's that beau of yours," I retorted with scorn. "What is he, anyway, a writer, a religious fanatic, or a car racer?" At this my sister lashed out, and in the middle of Ocean Avenue we came to blows, scratching each other's cheeks, pulling each other's hair, behaving like wildcats.

Each time I remember this scene I am amazed at how seriously we took our roles as prospective artist's wives. Though we ourselves were solemnly dedicated to our professions, it was essential that the men we marry be anything but dilettantes. We were, of course, following in our mother's footsteps and were probably pretentious. We had opinions about everything, from Walt Disney (*Fantasia*, we declared, was not art, nor did we approve of the music of Wagner or Sibelius), to Tchelitchew, whom Sylvia called Pavlitch; from W. H. Auden, whose poems we knew by heart, to Truman Capote, who, I noticed with distress, was my age and already famous. If our suitors had the same taste as we, this had something to do with love. Since we were not altogether certain about our own genius, we would have to be convinced of theirs.

Perhaps genius is commensurate with the size of one's ego. Bobby, the art student I presently married, was at least sure of himself, which made my part as artist's wife easier to play, for nothing is more difficult than propping up a faltering ego. Sylvia's young man, however, decided to become a monk, to leave the burden of greatness to God rather than shoulder it himself. This left Sylvia with the difficult task of proving herself the genius, and she has struggled manfully all her life with a career that, in newspaper articles and photographs, made her appear intense and self-assured. I admire her for this, knowing the private agonies — the self-doubt, the loneliness — involved.

I myself let my husband do the work. Not unlike my mother, I have become the handmaiden of genius. It is a fussy, tyrannical, indiscreet role. One tiptoes by the studio door. Is he working or reading the papers? He seems depressed; things are not going well. Perhaps he needs a model. I'll find him a pretty one, young, not too plump. I musn't mention the bills. I will cook something delicious and keep the children quiet. Why isn't he producing more? I keep expecting him to reward my devotion with a continuous production of masterpieces for my entertainment. But he proceeds with slow, sensitive, brooding perfectionism. There are no accidents involved. Each move is premeditated, perfectly executed, in sharp contrast to my father's impulsive bravura performances, which alternated with total failure. Then Mother would slip into the studio, pick up a brush, and say, "Here, let me show you," causing an outburst of rage. Often he would mull over her criticism and, without admitting it, follow her advice. Wise enough not to gloat over her triumph in his presence, she could not resist boasting to me with impish satisfaction, "The trouble is, I am always right. No wonder I drive him crazy."

I have played the part differently, never entering the studio unless invited, never criticizing unless asked. But this tactic, too, has its drawbacks. "You're not really interested in what I do," has been my husband's melancholy complaint. Or, when after watching him read the papers until noon, I say imprudently, "You're wasting the whole morning," he will storm out with suppressed fury, and I will have ruined his mood for the day.

My son Christian, the painter, also took his role seriously from an early age, and here again a mother has to proceed with circumspection, admiring but never prodding, understanding but never assuming. For although he is dedicated to the increasingly vague and elusive pursuit of art, the number of its practitioners has proliferated. This makes the profession seem less convincing, a kind of decadent self-indulgence. *Creativity* has become a dubious word, often confused with therapy, and art has become both less functional and more commercial, more histrionic, so that the only sure way to be noticed in the crowd is to have genius. But how can one ever be sure it is the real thing?

After Father died, Mother became possessed by his genius. "How about you?" I'd say, irritated by this sudden hero worship. "You're a sculptor too, after all." I wondered if it was modesty or insecurity that caused this. Or perhaps to be freed of him she had first to build a monument to his memory.

"Oh, but I'm not important. I'm nothing compared to him." Her conversations now all began with, "As Joep used to say. . . ," and she collected a group of young artists about her to whom she constantly held him up as an example. They, naturally, found him old-fashioned. "He's had his day," they said. "It's our turn now." Their heroes ranged from contemporary Hindu sages to such highly visible public figures as Andy Warhol. They were, however, fascinated with her and, if she had been willing to play the part, would probably have considered her a genius.

Determined to enroll me in her campaign to publicize my father, she relentlessly pursued Dutch publishers for three years, until she found one willing to commission a biography of him lavishly illustrated with colored reproductions. Two foundations agreed to finance the project; I would be the author.

I was delighted but apprehensive. Whose life would I be writing, my father's or her husband's?

As I proceeded with my research, Mother always at my side prompting me, pointing out to me how inferior everyone else's work was to his, I built up a wall of resistance. She drove me through every nook and cranny of Holland, over polders, along rivers, to abandoned churches where we retrieved rusty keys from former nuns or retired priests. We were shown their gardens, served cups of tea as they reminisced. "He had very good cigars," said the priests. "He was generous with his wine." Many times we got lost when, on a hunch, Mother would dart off down a byway.

"I think this is where there is an early abstract window. No, where is it? Perhaps the church was torn down, or perhaps it was bombed in the war, or perhaps it was in another province altogether."

We saw windows in the stairwells of factories, in breweries, hospitals, city halls, high schools, museums, private homes. And always there was Mother's commentary: "Look how hideous that man's work is compared to Joep's. No sense of color, awkward, pretentious."

Occasionally I got away on the sly to visit his former colleagues, his school friends, and, much against her wish, his two brothers. "There's nothing they can tell you that I don't know," she said, looking hurt. What was she afraid of? What would they divulge?

His older brother Charles had grown deaf, which made communication difficult. A leonine athlete, swarthy, with a

star-shaped scar on his cheek, he had always seemed to me
a kind of Heathcliff, with a romantic temper and violent
rages. He had spent his youth mining for diamonds in
Africa, had become a Resistance leader during the war, and
later was briefly a government inspector of coal mines.
After his retirement he built furniture out of weathered
oak, copies of antiques that were works of art. But something always went sour; he invested badly and felt wronged
by society. As we talked, his resentment of Father's success
became evident. "They always talk about him as the great
painter," he complained. "As if that were the most important thing. He was a damn nice fellow and a generous host."

Father's younger brother Edmond was terminally ill and
in a hospital. I found him lying in a room with a view of the
garden, a large and handsome man with a gray beard.
"One does not choose one's own destiny," he mused philosophically. He talked with affection of the brother who had
preceded him. "We were very close as boys." I could tell that
Mother, as well as fame and career, had come between
them, and that he considered them both to be intruders.
"Fame," he smiled with a grand gesture toward the
flowerbeds outside. "One must learn to take it with a touch
of irony." I was inclined to agree with him. He was himself a
man of no mean accomplishment, with several witty novels
to his name.

My misgivings about writing "De Book," as Mother
called it, grew. Would it not be ridiculous for a daughter to
praise her father's work without reservation? Yet if I did
not, would my mother ever forgive me?

She now took me to see a church that was decorated
entirely with windows made by four generations of Nic-
olases: my great-grandfather, grandfather, father, sister,
and cousin. I had read the correspondence dealing with
the Apocalypse windows that Father had made there in the
fifties. The subject matter had awed him. "I feel that in this
project I can achieve the high point of my entire career. I

have to compete with the famous French tapestries and with Mr. Dürer." In those days he fell asleep night after night over Revelations, obsessed by visions in his dreams.

The church was a somber brick neo-Gothic of no particular distinction. In the nave were Great-Grandfather's traditional windows, more or less pre-Raphaelite, saints in niches with patterned borders appropriate to the architecture. My sister's windows, much freer and very much in Father's style, were decorative and monumental. I observed all this with critical approval, pen in hand, as Mother explained who had done what, how the church had become a foundation called *Four Generations,* and that it attracted many tourists.

Then I turned to Father's windows, which covered the nave to the right. There, lit by the setting sun behind them, was a series of wildly agitated scenes: vast crowds and angry dragons with pointed teeth, fierce angels flying about blowing their trumpets, gyrating birds, armies holding forests of spears, a king with a sword in his mouth and eyes of fire, monsters and prophets, and, charging across a host of prostrate bodies and skeletons, the four horsemen. All of this was depicted in a bold counterpoint of color, so grand and ambitious in scale that it took my breath away. At that moment I was convinced. "It's genius, all right," I muttered under my breath, too overwhelmed to worry about whether Mother was wearing her "I-told-you-so" expression.

From then on, neither my opinion nor hers mattered; the book wrote itself. Perhaps this is the final test of genius—that all opinions are overruled and we suspend judgment, allowing ourselves to be carried away. For the same thing must have happened to the artist. Something larger must have taken hold of him, a visionary madness overriding rationality.

Here in his windows of the Apocalypse, Father's vision had matched St. John's, and Mother had been right.

20
TRAVELS WITH SUZANNA THE DIVER

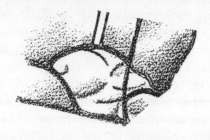

My mother sighs loudly. She sits crushed between young people wearing torn blue jeans, retrieving cheese sandwiches from their backpacks, in a Dutch train going to Paris. Obviously, my argument about trains being more restful than automobiles does not hold water and I feel guilty. We have already changed once, carrying the elaborate luggage that holds her elegant wardrobe up and down stairs between windy platforms. Seats have been hard to find, too, but then this has been her fault to some extent. Though she is seventy-five, it is hard to impress people with the fact that she is a frail, elderly widow to be treated with consideration. Her most constant expression is one of flirtatious astonishment, and she darts about with the agility of a squirrel.

Having recently seen the films *Murder on the Orient Express* and *Julia*, I had told her I was determined to recapture the romance of the great trains. This was really a ruse on my part, to avoid being driven by her all the way from Holland to Italy, for though she drives competently if in strange darts and spurts, she never seems to know where she is going and uses a birdlike instinct rather than maps. Now, in my middle age, it is my turn to take her on a trip, to lead the way, sit in the driver's seat figuratively if not literally, as she has always done.

I underestimate her resilience, of course. In no time at all she is talking animatedly in three different languages to everyone in the compartment, cocking her head, charming them with wide-eyed attentiveness. When it is time to change trains again, her mysterious money bag, which she had been carrying in a bulge against her heart, is left lying on the seat. How it ever landed there, fat with various wads of foreign moneys she retrieved from odd hiding places all over her house, remains a mystery. In any case, everyone in the compartment now points to it and exclaims, "I think you forgot something!"

I scold her maternally but she laughs herself silly, saying, "That's what happens when I try to be too clever."

In the next train she promptly falls asleep, waking up once in a while to comment, outraged, "Hey, I've been sleeping. I never sleep on trains."

"Are you sisters?" someone asks. How often I have been plagued with this question, from childhood until now, when we both have gray hair. Never mind. We love each other with a fierce, complicated love that often resembles mutual tyranny. Hers is rightful, since she is my mother and therefore entitled to tell me how to cross the street or comb my hair; mine is a tyranny based mostly on size. I tower over her, probably twice as much in my imagination as in actuality. But behind her look of unassuming modesty she hides an iron will. To me, this amounts to cheating. A strong woman ought not to hide behind all that artifice, and so I have a way of barging in and saying what I think. I also have a growing urge to protect her, to organize her, as if she were an ineffectual child. She has always provoked this tendency in her older sisters, Jeanne and Maria, as well. As a result, she insists on absolute independence. She carries her own bags and knows exactly how to manage her affairs, but requires a large meal every two hours to restore her amazing energy.

We are on our way, via Paris, to Forte dei Marmi, where a friend has lent me her summer villa for the off-season. Forte dei Marmi . . . all my life I have had to listen to my mother's stories about the idyllic summer she spent there during World War I, about the fourteen boyfriends with whom she fished, swam, and sailed all day long. Now I am taking her to revisit times past with as much nostalgia for those stories as she herself must feel for her actual youth, as if we were seeing reality in mirrors endlessly reflecting each other.

In Paris we stop for two days to see my daughter Stephanie, a dancer, perform. When we arrive at her apartment, she has already left for the theater, but her photograph, on posters, is on every streetcorner. "She lives in this street and she is very *gentille,*" says the baker's wife. I am awed, feeling as if my daughter were really my mother, someone important and intimidating. She towers over me, so that now I seem to be both my mother's mother and my daughter's daughter. It occurs to me that we are like those Russian dolls that fit inside one another, the mother inside her daughter inside her daughter.

At the theater I am greeted with exclamations of *"la maman de Stephanie!"* and we are ushered to the best seats in the house. The minute she appears on stage I realize she is a star and I am suddenly terrified. It is as if she had become the victim of a demanding monster, the public, and I am a helpless witness to her sacrifice. I am terribly moved and clap and shout myself hoarse in the hope of carrying the rest of the audience along. But Mother seems detached, cool. She has always had what one calls "good taste," the most arbitrary of qualities. Is she going to apply it critically to this very modern, wild, free form of dancing? I decide to ignore her and sail with my enthusiasm intact backstage to be enfolded in the long, sinewy arms of my exhausted child. "It's the most original thing I ever saw," I rave. Delighted, she says, "I always knew you were the best critic."

My tiny mother has disappeared somewhere into the background and I too am soon lost in the press of movie stars, impresarios, large men in fur coats, and perspiring dancers that follows her to her dressing room. What is a dancer's mother's function exactly? I wonder, watching the square, red-headed mother of the other "star" silently packing, cleaning, folding tights and leotards. It is rather like being an artist's wife, after all. The two stars embrace their bouquets of roses, take large swigs of slivovitz from the bottle, and gobble chocolates, complaining all the while of nausea and colitis. I am about to comment on their diet with motherly disapproval but think better of it.

Two days of this reflected glory exhausts me, because my mother insists on staying up to share the nightlife of the stars, thus frustrating my efforts to convince Stephanie to get some rest. At exotic nightclubs as secret as speakeasies, we meet important persons. Whenever I open my mouth to make what I think is inoffensive small talk, Stephanie kicks me under the table, frowning meaningfully.

"I can't help it," she apologizes later. "I always think you're going to say the wrong thing." Oh, the guilt mothers inflict on their daughters! How endlessly complex our relationships! Since she has given us her bed, Stephanie sleeps on a couch, then rushes off to classes and rehearsals while we try to be helpful, washing dishes and tights. I worry and fret about her health. "And what about *life*? She has absolutely no life of her own!" But my mother pooh-poohs this cliché of mine with remarkable wisdom. "Don't be silly," she says. "She's an artist doing what she wants to do."

Mother convinces me that we are just in the way, and so we go on an expedition to cash some Eurochecks with which, she assures me, we are very rich. The first bank we go to, however, will not touch them. "These have expired," they say. "They're no longer valid."

"What do you mean?" Mother asks. "They've always worked."

"They're green, and now they should be blue. Try another bank, you'll see." At the next bank everyone is out for lunch except for some inexperienced young girls, who give us lots of money for the green checks, though they say they've never heard of their like.

As soon as Mother has pocketed the money, she gives me a sharp look and says, "Let's get out of here." She runs as inconspicuously as possible to the next corner and leans against a building. "My knees are trembling," she says. "That man was right. I remember now that these checks are not the right ones. But I gave them the telephone number of my bank so I don't think it's really dishonest, do you? They'll collect their money. But let's keep walking, they might find out and send the police."

Arm in arm with my mother, the bank robber, we now visit Beaubourg, which, except for the jugglers and fire-eaters on the square in front, she decides is in "very bad taste."

Our train leaves that evening from the Gare de Lyon, the echoing station with its coming and going of luggage carts, its bells announcing arrivals and departures, its crowds of passengers en route to the Riviera or the Orient. All this epitomizes my great expectations of travel.

We settle in our sleeping compartment, a courteous valet in attendance. With childlike satisfaction I examine the small sink, the pieces of soap, the cabinet holding a carafe of cool water, when suddenly a tall, slim figure dressed in a long coat appears on the platform. It is Stephanie, my dancing daughter, a scarf flung over her shoulders, her

hennaed hair curled in the latest fashion. She has not slept
all night, too tired to be able to relax, but has now run out
during an hour off between rehearsals to wave good-bye to
us, the way one is supposed to wave at the Gare de Lyon, as
if the departing ones were leaving on an endless, final
voyage. It seems this way each time I leave her, and my heart
sinks as the train pulls out.

On our way through the French countryside, glued to
our window until the last shred of sun goes down, Mother
says, *"La douce France. . . ."* She offers such comments timidly, as if afraid I will violently disagree, a thing I am likely
to do at the drop of a hat. This diplomatic tentativeness of
hers makes me feel guilty. It means, "Who am I to be
literary? You're the writer after all. I must respect your
ego." She knows my ego only too well and tiptoes around it,
the way I will forgive Stephanie any amount of kicking
under the table. But even a mother's indulgence can be
irritating. "Yes," I nod. *"La douce France."* Why not?

The next morning we are in Florence. We check our
luggage and begin to walk. At Santa Maria Novella, Mass is
being said in a dark corner and we wander over to what
Mother insists are Ghirlandaio's frescoes. "I remember
Professor Fasola explaining them to us. It was sixty years
ago." She is right, of course; nothing one learns at fifteen is
ever forgotten. We buy freesias at the flower market for the
friend who is lending us the house in Forte. On the
Lungarno, we climb up to her fourth-floor apartment. My
friend Suzy, who is also the daughter of my mother's friend
Costanza and the granddaughter of Professor Fasola, gives
us a lunch of spinach and poached eggs, served by an
Ethiopian woman wearing a red and gold turban.

"What a nice painting," says my mother.

"I wish I knew who painted it," says Suzy, "but since my
mother died, nobody remembers anything."

"I know, I can tell you." My mother does not hesitate. "It's
a Miss Chapin. I remember her well." Suzy smiles,

delighted with this voice from the past. We are given the key to the house in Forte and take the three o'clock train.

It is a slow local, full of students and peasants. One of them comes from Seravezza, a village in the mountains above Forte. "Would you happen to know a Mr. Tonino F. there?" my mother asks.

"Why, of course," he says. "He is always in the piazza discussing with the pharmacist."

"Could you give him a message from Suzanna the Diver?" She writes a few words on a piece of paper. "I hear he's gotten fat." She sighs. I vaguely remember the dashing young man who came to visit us in Holland when I was a child, one of the fourteen boyfriends.

Sixty years, she explains. It has been sixty years ago. They are properly impressed. "Forte is much more beautiful now, you'll see," they assure her. "The hotels, the beach cabins." But she shakes her head sadly.

"It's impossible. How about the white oxen that pulled the carts loaded with marble down to the pier? How about the sailboats?"

Ah, no, they agree. No more oxen. But the elegance, the *passeggiata* along the beach, the villas, and the tennis courts! They get us a taxi and carry our luggage. "How nice Italians are," we remark, and then my mother's homing instinct goes to work. "Here we go left, and then straight for a while. Where has the *pineta* gone? And here to the right. It has changed, but not that much, after all. There is the sea. . . ." The taxi stops. We push the gate in the high garden wall and turn the key in the lock.

The house was built at the beginning of the century in the style of a Tuscan farmhouse, with red-tiled floors and thick walls. There are white slipcovers over the sofas and ancient oak tables and chests. Professor Fasola had been a Tolstoian and only a peasant style would do. Pointing to the art-nouveau-style villa across the street, my mother says, "That was considered corrupt. We were not allowed to look

at it. Here in the corner under the stairs we used to sit and
talk all day. Then we'd be scolded—'don't sit there doing
nothing, keep busy'—so we'd fetch our embroidery. But my
sister Maria and Costanza were always whispering secrets.
They were such a nuisance. For tea we'd eat bread and salt.
There was little food during the war, so bread and salt
seemed delicious."

It is early April and the weather is unsettled. I am
awakened by the voices of gardeners. One of them sits in a
tree right outside my window, shaving it of all its branches.
The lawn is covered with tiny daisies and several blackbirds
are singing their hearts out. I run to the beach across the
street, miles and miles of sand being raked by a single man.
Another man is peacefully painting posts and greets me as
if he has known me all my life. He expresses the desire for
warmer weather. A black dog plays among the deserted
rows of cabins. Turning back to the house, I see the mountains in the distance, huge crags with strange white pools
on them. Snow? Impossible. It is cool but full spring; the
cherry trees are blooming and ripe oranges glow behind
garden walls.

"How dare you go to the beach without me?" Mother
complains when I bring her breakfast in bed, even though I
know there is nothing she detests more.

The Grand Hotel, the boardinghouses are closed and
the people in the street are taking it easy. Stores open
sporadically, except on weekends, when the *passeggiata* is in
full swing along the pier. Then visitors from Lucca and
Florence, dressed to the teeth, parade up and down past
the elegant boutiques eating ice cream, buying balloons,
dining at tables tentatively set outside, watching their children ride around on ponies or go-carts, indulging themselves in shameless Italian fashion.

I find Italian Sundays melancholy and suggest we take a
bus to the hills. "Seravezza!" says my mother hopefully.
Contrary, I insist on Pietra Santa, famed home of bronze

foundries. "That should interest you, since you're a sculptor," I argue.

"It'll be closed on Sunday." But I am stubborn. When we get to the piazza I lead the way along a rampart bordered with plane trees.

"Where are you going? Not so fast, I want to see the church," Mother complains, but I am drawn toward the heights, the terraced olive groves, emerald green under the silver branches. Wild primroses, anemones, violets are blooming on the embankments. The hairpin road now climbs steeply and my mother is getting cross, a bit out of breath, when a car containing a man and a small boy stops. "Are you going to Capriglia? Can I give you a ride?" Yes, yes, I say, and we jump in.

"I'll tell you what," says the driver, who smells strongly of wine. "I'll take you to my house, best view anywhere. . . Italy is not what it used to be. Terrible what's going on. I'm a very expansive type, I like to share, my house is yours, I'll give you the keys."

"It's in a chestnut forest, all ours," says the child. "There are records. You can play Beethoven."

"Best tortellini in Italy are made in Capriglia. Foreigners come. Americans build villas that cost a million. But my house is quiet. In it you can forget the rottenness of Italy."

I wish he would keep his hands on the wheel as the road weaves back and forth, up and away.

"You must be Swedish. Aren't you Swedish?"

Mother explains our nationality, our relationship. "Ah," he says, looking back dangerously. "But you're very well preserved."

A bit too friendly, I think, but his house is worth it. The little boy skips ahead along the muddy path, brandishing Papa's keys. "Three hundred steps and you're there!" A modest cabin, perched on a promontory, a pergola overlooking a steep valley, the coastal plain, the glistening sea. "You must come at night and see the lights!" The plum tree and rosemary are blooming. He must show us the beds, the record player, "and the outhouse, in case you want to do peepee." Chairs are pulled out, bottles of wine uncorked, Beethoven played, as father and son expend themselves, chatter away. "I'll take you home in my car. I could show you Viareggio. You must taste the tortellini. We'll have a party and I'll turn on the colored lights on the pergola."

Increasingly ill at ease, I stop Mother just as she is about to give him our address.

"We must go, our husbands are waiting," I say, feeling that matrimony will protect us. When at last we step onto the bus back to Forte, I heave a sigh of relief.

Italian men haven't changed, we decide, and Mother once more reminisces. "One young man stood waiting at the streetcorner every day for a whole month when I was fifteen. He followed me wherever I went. When I got angry he protested, 'But, signorina, I'm of very good family.'"

"How about the fourteen boyfriends? Were they not that way?" I ask.

"Oh, no. That was much more fun. We fished and sailed and swam. I was one of the gang."

"Were they the ones who called you Suzanna the Diver?"

"You saw the pier, didn't you? High, isn't it? They taught me to dive off those little boats, then I dared them to dive off the pier. None of them would, but I did. From then on they called me *La Tuffatrice*, the diver."

Every day there were more memories: how she would escape through the upstairs window to go swimming in the moonlight; how Professor Fasola had taken her for long walks to talk about philosophy — "And you know, all I can remember is longing for an ice cream." One evening she had to get all dressed up to go out with one of her boyfriends, "so I could reassure the girl he was in love with that he behaved himself like a gentleman. I hear he has become very rich," she adds wistfully. She must have used her guilelessness even then to resist the seductive instincts of young Italians.

Wherever we go, Mother draws — quick, illustrative sketches. The peasant women in black hang out of their windows and watch her, this agile little woman as old as they in years yet so unlike them. I love their weathered, leathery look, their hair tied in knots, their massive old age. I point them out to Mother and say, "Why can't you look like them?"

She takes no offense, smiles serenely. "You've wanted me to look like that ever since you were a little girl," she says. Is it just that I long to have her disappear as a rival? I don't think so. I want her to be enormously solid, wise, "above" me, but she insists on remaining right by my side, offering me all the intimacies of her life, its girlish frivolities rather than its mature insights. On the bus descending from Collonata she dodges nervously from side to side, hiding below the window in terror of precipices, overhanging rocks, dizzying turns. When she finally descends with a sigh of relief, a huge, red-faced peasant who has been sitting behind her throws her a kiss, which she accepts with delight. "What is it about me?" she says impishly.

Whenever I react by becoming motherly, even patronizing, she makes it quite clear that this is not my role, claiming for herself the privilege of serving me, just as I longed to serve Stephanie. I must not get tired, carry bags of food, do the dishes, or catch cold. In fact, she must buy me a woolen undershirt. I stubbornly refuse, resent every minute spent in shops, long to take another bus to another hill town. She says, "You're just like Bonne Maman. As a tourist she was insatiable." But Bonne Maman would never have fit inside her daughter, being rather large, and I do not want to play my game of Russian dolls with her. Yet here is this trait of hers that I have apparently inherited. It is disconcerting.

We go to Seravezza, but Tonino, the boyfriend of sixty years ago, is not "discussing" with the pharmacist on the piazza today. We are told he has fled the rainy spring and gone to Florence. Mother now begins to make daily pilgrimages to the public telephones in the hope of reaching him, but he is not in the book. "I remember he had a married sister who always ordered her shoes from Paris, but what was her name?" she frets. So we go to Lucca and wander through its medieval streets. It begins to pour. My mother finds an umbrella outside a store, picks it up, and walks off with it. A young man comes out of the store and looks at her with some astonishment. "Is it yours?" she asks innocently.

"That's all right," he says. "You need it more than I do."

So now the bank robber has become an umbrella thief. At a stylish restaurant she is finally able to eat a long-remembered dish, baby goat with polenta, but it is not quite as delicious as she had thought. In fact, she is now talking less about Forte sixty years ago than about her many succeeding travels.

At the market she says, "In Brittany we ate our peas with scallions." On the beach, "In Greece, tourists swam naked on our island." And out of the blue, while waiting for a bus, she volunteers, "Mexico City is like Brussels. The Indians all wanted to touch my hair." Her digressions destroy my total absorption in this place, making of us ordinary tourists as her mother had been, here one day, there the next. The rows of villas in Forte do, after all, have a touch of California about them, where Bonne Maman died alone in a nursing home.

In Querceta, we go to the race of the donkeys. Pushing our way through the crowds, we stand for an hour craning our necks, Mother becoming the publicly appointed arbiter of who should take off his hat so as not to obscure the view, and who should stop pushing and stepping on toes. Finally, exhausted, we leave before the reluctant donkeys begin their race and walk home along winding back roads among olive groves, orchards, and vineyards. Holiday crowds gathered in farmyards greet us with, "Long live the Oak, the Frog, the Boar!" — these being the various factions of the donkey race.

Sometimes I bicycle along these paths, feeling a need for independence. Then my mother walks down to the beach or sketches the flower vendors in the piazza, the fisherman with baskets of tiny shells. When she comes home, she makes strange statements: "I was walking along the mall. There was a dog with pointed orange ears. Everyone looked at it. I think it was the devil."

We take one more bus to the highest possible village, Stazzemo. It has been raining and shreds of mists cling to the mountains. A torrent of white marble dust dashes down to the valley, and everywhere are tumbling, toppling rocks that have been burrowed into by the drills and saws at the quarries. We reach Stazzemo in the evening. The bus stops below the town on a promontory with an old church and a cemetery. How removed, how idyllic it seems, but we barely have time to walk up to the piazza and then turn back before the bus departs again and brings us down to earth.

It is now our last day. An icy rain clatters down on the desolate streets of our summer resort. In the evening, as we go for a farewell walk on the beach, the sky clears. The sun comes out in streaks and we can see Capriglia, Capezzano, Seravezza, and Pietra Santa, but Stazzemo remains invisible. Perhaps it doesn't exist after all, but is a figment of our imaginations, the way certain memories too become blurred, doubtful.

As our train approaches Paris, where Mother will get off to return to Holland, she suddenly sits down on the bed where she has been sleeping, as if her knees have buckled as they did when she ran away from the bank in Paris. "Now it's all over," she says. "It has been nice. When will I see you again?" She looks so lost sitting there that I remember myself as an eleven-year-old girl going back to convent school after the holidays, saying good-bye, having to swallow tears without showing they are there. Why is she returning to her lonely house in my father's country, where she has always been considered a foreigner? Why am I speeding on to take a flight back to New York? Why is my daughter not there to greet us on the quay of the station, waving her veil scarf with her long dancer's arms? She has flown to Tulsa, Oklahoma, to dance, and from there will fly back to Paris, then on to Tokyo. It occurs to me that if the tourist in all three of us comes from Bonne Maman, it is from Suzanna the Diver that Stephanie and I have inherited this fierce independence, this refusal to claim anything from the other, leaving us all free to lead separate lives, meeting now and then to watch each other perform, to embrace, and then to wave good-bye.

21
THE WOMAN
WHO LOST
HER HEAD

There are long periods of time, stretches of years, decades in fact, during which I think it has happened, that I belong, that this land is mine, that the weeds have adopted me. I return to my parents' house over there, in Limburg, and with judgmental detachment find the air stale, the people provincial, the mental climate claustrophobic, the Catholic church overbearing and sad, the land cramped, the brick dark and gloomy. Thank God, I think, I have shed it, the old skin that clung to me like a parasite.

Then there occurs one of those strange immigrant phenomena that makes me realize it is impossible.

It was early spring when I lost my head, having just returned from Holland, where my mother had almost died. "Don't come!" she had said over the telephone, trying to sound matter-of-fact and totally in control. "Either you'll be too late or I'll survive. In either case I shall not need you." It took me a few days to get over my irritation at not being needed; then, of course, I went.

Perhaps I flattered myself that I reconnected her intense, bony head to the world around her. I had performed this operation by reading to her from *Remembrance of Things Past* as she lay in the pleasant hospital room from which she could oversee the whole village. Two days before I had witnessed from her window a wild and surprisingly atavistic carnival parade as she lay writhing in agony. Now the curtains were closed, the lights dimmed, and the body, returned from intensive care, lay still and passive, stuck about with tubes and intravenous needles.

The book, which I had picked at random from her shelves, fell open at the passage where Swann first visits Odette in her apartment, which she has decorated with chrysanthemums. As I read, the chrysanthemums in this hospital room began to glow, their art nouveau designs incandescent, their bittersweet perfume heady. Then Mother thanked me, asked me to stop, slept, and convalesced.

One convalesces quite easily at the age of seventy-nine nowadays; then life continues as before. Somehow the garden gets planted, the pig farmer and the baker's wife drop in, Carnival is followed by Lent. Dressed in an Oriental robe and Guatemalan stockings, Suzanna the Diver peered out the window at her neighbor's children on bicycles and mused philosophically, "I am fortunate in life always to have liked simple people."

No longer needed, I returned home.

Now, here I was, well into my fifties, losing my head on the living room floor after a peculiarly soothing massage applied by a young man with a forceful manner. As he lifted my arms and legs, then dropped them as if they were weightless, I had grown totally unaware of my body; I no longer seemed to inhabit it but to float above it. Then he had taken my head carefully in his hands and moved it around in various directions. I had the distinct impression that it had fallen off, and I began to giggle uncontrollably.

The young man was called Willem and came, by coincidence, from Limburg, my father's province. He had passed through Long Island with an international acting company and, naked, painted black, had performed the part of Orestes in Greek, as well as that of a sea gull in Portuguese. The local university had solicited beds for the actors, and aware of my country of origin, had sent me a Dutchman.

Swarthy, with prominent cheekbones and green, animal eyes, Willem moved with energetic grace and a histrionic gift for gesture that was curiously reminiscent of the figures in my father's paintings. With a musical, deep-throated voice like that of the "Prince of Poets" who had frequented my parents' house by the sea when I was a child, he spoke the first language I had ever learned and had almost forgotten. The words rose out of another time, another existence, and since no one, neither my husband nor my sons, could understand them, the young man began to have a tremendous hold on me. As I did with Mr. Pimput so many years ago, we talked about poetry and the meaning of existence, about longing and the elusiveness of love, all in that other language learned at a time before I had acquired a strong and rather well-organized head.

When the performances ended, Willem defected from his acting company and announced that he was going to conquer New York. He didn't seem to be in any particular hurry to start his campaign, however, and began to organize our household instead. "You, sir, may improvise on your guitar after dinner for an hour while I do the dishes."

My husband was touched, and shyly began to pick at the strings of a guitar he had neglected for some twenty-five years, but pretty soon he fell asleep. Willem looked at him, puzzled and slightly saddened. "Why does he sleep?" he asked. "He should play more."

An actor in the true sense of the word, Willem took action, and whether he was sweeping the floor or cooking

himself up a terrible mess of eggs, onions, and mush-
rooms, his actions had a deliberateness that was invigorat-
ing. My life seemed to begin anew. In fact, an unexplainable happiness filled me that was very like love. The
house, seen through Willem's eyes, breathed a clear beauty,
the music we played had a new significance, the sheets we
folded together were tauter, smoother than they had ever
been. This compatriot of mine was a companion unlike a
son, unlike a husband, but with a strong link, I realized, to
the father whom I had never quite approached across the
formal distance of the generation gap. Now here he was
reincarnated, not as an older man locked in his secrets
whom a daughter can only guess at and follow from a
distance like those women who had followed Christ,
washed His feet in oil, accompanied Him to the cross, and
then, finding the tomb empty, learned He had escaped
them. This young man was like the man whose life I had
relived as I wrote my father's biography, full of hopes,
energy, mystical yearnings, and illogical fantasies.

What he had come to do here was still unclear, except
that it included someday winning the Nobel Prize. The
candor of this arrogance, revealed as we tramped together
through the countryside for hours on end, was somehow
irresistible. How could I tell him about the difficulty of it,
the frustration that awaited him? Emotions flitted constantly across his face, ranging from the ebullient to the
tragic, yet he maintained a kind of reserve, a personal
dignity that I respected. What my father expressed
through drawing or painting on glass, Willem stylized in
gesture, in the way he transformed his surroundings into
scenery, imposing an aesthetic control over lawns, rooms,
tabletops.

"What am I? I don't know," he'd say, and change his hat
or his coat or grow a beard.

After he had grown three beards and shaved them off
again, my husband asked, irritated, "When is he leaving?"

And so I drove him to the train with his saxophone, his didgeridoo, and his personal manifesto, called *The Art of Lying*. Two red-winged blackbird wings were sewn onto his hat.

Then the house returned to its somnolent routine, and with the advance of spring, a weed emerged by my front stoop.

I remembered its origin. The previous autumn, during her last visit before her illness, my mother had taken it upon herself to clean my front steps, the little terrace, the cracks between the flagstones. The thoroughness of her brushing, scraping, and weeding had been an exercise in space control, a Zen meditation on orderliness. I had noticed Willem cleaning my kitchen in the same way, every fork aligned, every surface emptied, wiped clean. He had also cut down a tree, split the logs, and stacked them in a perfect pyramid by the back door, creating a precise structure.

"What a haphazard, messy nation we Americans have created," I said at breakfast, but my husband was not amused and grew defensive.

"We're not fussy, if that's what you mean," he said. I did not answer him but glanced out the window at the one weed between the cracks of the slate.

"I'll leave it," Mother had said with a gesture that implied artistic judgment. "One weed. You're allowed that."

How healthy it seemed now, quite elegant even, with its long narrow leaves and dark spine. As I wondered daily what Willem might be up to, I looked at my weed and saw it branch out and grow tall and lush, with something like buds forming at its extremities. What would it become?

Meanwhile, in New York, remarkable spectacles were being organized, actors rounded up by the dozen wearing feather boas, carrying baskets full of chickens, and at eight A.M. one day, at Battery Park, a reenactment of the landing of Columbus featured Willem with his saxophone arriving by rowboat from the Statue of Liberty.

This was described to me in glowing terms over the telephone. "But Willem," I asked, "was there an audience?"

"At eight o'clock in the morning? Don't be silly."

"And what are you doing for money?" An ominous silence followed.

"Yes, well, that's a bit of a problem," he had to admit. He was sleeping on someone's kitchen floor and learning how to fast. "One doesn't really need to eat," he assured me with bravado. The next time he called, however, the bravado had disappeared.

"Isn't your friend going to throw you out of his kitchen?"

"As a matter of fact, he already has."

"And are you still fasting?"

"I take advantage of women," he said. "I'm shameless."

"Can't you find work?"

"Ah, but we're doing a show. It will be very good. You must come. I'm playing Professor van der Kunst, an art critic who devastates SoHo. Also Columbus, of course, and the sea gull. We have a theater for one night."

I went to see the spontaneous, zany spectacle and laughed till I cried, but I was the sole spectator in the small theater.

"Didn't you advertise?" I asked.

"Hell, no," he said. "We're doing it for ourselves." But the young actors, dancers, and musicians he had gathered around him now surrounded him in protest. "We've got to be paid!" they cried. "We're tired of doing shows without scripts. This is all too disorganized. We're not just playing games."

And yet their performance had been more original, offered more visionary delights than anything I had seen in years.

I lent Willem the cash I had in my purse and returned to Long Island, where my weed received me at the doorstep, vigorous and lanky, now separated into three different branches. It promised to produce something unexpected and new and I watched it grow with unexplainable tenderness.

"It's getting out of hand," said my husband. It meant nothing to him. How could I explain that it was my mother's saving it that made it special? Like Willem, my irresponsible protégé, my impractical adventurer, it promised much but needed patient coaxing. "It's like an artist," I said.

I began to receive furious calls from a clever little actress whom Willem had befriended. "What is this?" she complained. "He sleeps in my bed, he eats my food, he won't look for a job like the rest of us, and now he tells me he has only one true love, the girl he left behind. Let him go back where he came from."

But to Willem, going back would mean defeat. He must somehow conquer New York, though his shoes were full of holes and it rained the entire month of May.

I found him a job with some enterprising tree men in my neighborhood. Desperate, Willem accepted. Once more he would be staying under our roof, and aware of the fact that my husband would be anything but delighted, I imagined I could hide him, providing him with a separate entrance, a hot plate for his coffee, a separate bathroom. He left every morning at the crack of dawn and returned late at night, but hiding Willem was like hiding an elephant. In fact, I now felt I was impersonating Babar's old lady, who tried to disguise her cumbersome pet as a dignified gentleman by dressing him in a pea-green suit.

With enthusiasm, Willem now surveyed the byways of Long Island from the top of a gigantic truck. I watched the three men ride off in the cool of the morning, their hair blowing in the wind, and waited impatiently with a sturdy hot meal late at night, when my husband was already asleep, for Willem's return. Then the day's adventure was described in glowing terms: the fine houses with swimming pools and stereos, ladies with elegant hairdos serving iced tea, glorious views over harbors and bays, the exotic fare bought at numerous delis along the way. The work he also saw in heroic terms: the swinging from ropes, the skill and courage of the tree surgeon, the enormous strength and energy of these "real Americans." But their obsession with work puzzled him. "They should play more," he said. "Work, work, why think only of work?" And yet, anxious not to be outdone, he too kept up an obsessive rhythm. Work became a theatrical event, an intense exertion, a preoccupation with the precise gesture, the constant flow of energy.

When my sons came home for weekends, they too seemed irritated by this newcomer. Try as I might, I could neither keep my elephant hidden nor understand why my family could not absorb him and be on perfectly friendly terms.

"Isn't he wearing my shoes?" asked one son.

"How long will he sleep in my bed?" asked the other, though he only dropped in every three months or so.

"You and your Dutch cousins," they both muttered chauvinistically when I burst out into childhood songs or delighted in odd expressions such as *yes-no-but* or exclaimed, "Willem, did you drink Klets as a child? You know, those bottles of water with a piece of licorice melted in them, and then you shook them up and sucked foam off the top?"

"Ja." He smiled, his mouth curling asymmetrically. "Ja. We used to let it set in a cool, dark place overnight."

My sons winced with embarrassment, but looking at Willem's skin, now dark brown from the Long Island sun, I could tell it had been nourished with Klets as my sons' had not. In spite of all that had intervened — the war, the Nazi occupation, the Beatles, Coca-Cola, pot, macrobiotics — Dutch children in summer still pulled foam from a bottle

full of black liquid kept cool in cellars or now, probably,
refrigerators.

My husband began to drink more than usual. He seemed
preoccupied and complained of fatigue, and all the while I
had new outbursts of energy. I painted the floor and cut the
lawn and wrote songs and translated long, obscure tracts
from the Dutch, and took my elephant swimming on weekends, and watched him pick out the most dazzling pair of
red wrestler's shoes. I became a willing audience as he
rehearsed a new "persona," an international Samurai made
up in Noh face with white paint and fierce, glistening eyes,
who was at the same time a Wall Street businessman
dressed in a three-piece suit. Our enormous shed, which
had appropriately always been called the Elephant House,
was now transformed into a circuslike stage set. Trapezes
decorated with quivering bells hung from the rafters, and
various ladders leaned against the walls. Willem would
scale these and then slide down them uttering loud guttural shouts, wielding both bamboo canes and an attaché
case while clouds of dust from the dirt floor rose dramat-
ically through shafts of sunlight.

Then one evening, a young girl called from Holland.
"Tell Willem I'll be arriving tomorrow at midnight."

Even I was a bit taken aback.

"It's her," he nodded. "I called her to come. She'll like it
here, it's so beautiful. Perhaps there will be a wedding," he
added dreamily. "She's like a queen. You will like her."

"But Willem," I said. "You didn't warn me. It's getting
rather crowded."

"Oh, I'll sleep on the floor. You'll see. She won't be any
trouble."

That morning I had gone to Mass. The sermon had been
about hospitality, about sharing what one has. I counted
my empty beds, measured the surrounding acres, and
thought of overcrowded little Holland, where vegetables
grow along the railroad tracks and squatters have

undisputed rights over every available empty corner. Of course there would be room for one more, I decided, though in no way would I be able to hide both Babar and his Celeste.

The girl was beautiful, quiet, and cheerful, and my men seemed to enjoy flirting with her. But they grew more and more menacing about Willem.

"Either he leaves or we do," they announced, confronting me. "He's taking over."

"But he's practically family," I pleaded.

"That's just a figment of your imagination."

"You have no idea how hard it is to start life in a new country. He has no working papers, no money."

"Then let him go back where he came from." How well I remembered that phrase being hurled at us refugees during the war. Through tears of frustration and regret I sat staring at my gangly weed, which had grown awkward and dusty during the last week, brushing against anyone trying to enter or leave the house with its top-heavy, coarse-looking buds. It was a dead, still, hot night, yet I had not heard Willem return from work. Now here he was, grimy, exhausted, looking down at me. He understood my distress at once.

"I have to leave, don't I?" he said. "Never mind. Don't worry about me."

"But where will you go?"

"Oh, perhaps we'll perform while floating up the Mississippi River on a raft. I'll be all right." He put his hand gently on my shoulder and added, "But you've got to keep fighting. It's your life you're fighting for."

By the next evening the two were gone, their room immaculately clean, the carpets beaten, the shelves dusted, the sheets washed and folded, the windows sparkling. How many American hippies had passed through the house leaving their beds unmade, their cameras forgotten (to be forwarded), their cigarette butts in the bathroom sink, their long hair in the tub? The only trace of Willem and his girl was an intense orderliness in the space they had briefly occupied.

My sons returned hungry from playing tennis, my husband came in from the studio whistling cheerfully, but instead of cooking dinner I sat on the front stoop feeling, for the first time, tired and alone in their midst. Then I noticed the emptiness where the weed had been. "Who cut it? Who cut it down?" I cried, outraged.

"I did," said my husband. "It was in the way."

"You had no right to. It was my weed! It meant something to me. I loved it just as much as the real plants, the ones that belong, the ones with names!" And as they all three looked down at me with astonishment, I realized they knew that I had lost it, my sensible, wise, controlled head. Now it would keep floating off along the highways and byways of drifting continents after a band of naked actors, neither quite sons nor brothers, painted black and spouting streams of meaningless language that was, nevertheless, a message urgently needed by the world.

22
LEAP YEARS

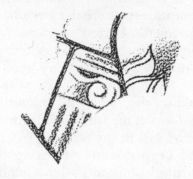

My mother is growing frail. She will not be with us forever. One of these days she will "leap over the fence," as she puts it. She continues to cultivate her garden, planting and gathering its many fruits, but behind its hedges, she tells me, wolves and jackals lurk.

To me, the intense plot of controlled nature that surrounds her house is real culture, but lately my mother has talked a lot about culture in that other sense, the way her own mother used to speak of it. "That is a very cultivated person," she will say, pursing her mouth a bit when she says *cul* and immediately I have visions of artifice, of cultured pearls and hothouse grapes, precious and pretentious. All it takes to deserve this compliment from her is a certain amount of name-dropping: Proust, Huxley, Bertrand Russell, Chagall, Dali, Zadkine. Anyone who loves Florence is cultivated. Automatically I rebel against this cultural snobbism. With typical contrariness, I champion weeds as opposed to controlled horticulture, refuse to teach my

214

children table manners, find Florence dark, oppressive, a ghetto for aesthetes.

Actually I suppose I am trying to keep Mother within her garden, to make of her that rooted grandmother who will strengthen my foothold on the world. I expect her to become passive, to simply be there, for this will make me freer to move about, knowing my roots are secure. But in spite of operations, dramatic brushes with the "wolves," her restless appetite for displacement remains undiminished.

"Perhaps I'll sell the house and move to Florence," she'll say, or "My last desire is to see Katmandu before I die."

"But think of the queer foods they eat. You wouldn't last a minute," I tell her.

"So what?" she says, then, only half resigned, she acquiesces. "Yes . . . perhaps those times are over."

But after I have bicycled energetically through fields of leeks, asparagus, and potatoes for several weeks I begin to long for some more civilized sights myself. I am determined, in particular, to show my husband two places that left a deep impression on me as a child. The first of these is in the far north of Holland, and since previously Mother has always led me south, preferably to Paris, that capital of culture, I seize the occasion of her indisposition during this holiday to explore Friesland.

"I understand. You'll have more fun without me," she says, looking forlorn.

"That's not true," I say. "But it's cold and windy there. It will be tiring."

"Tiring, tiring. You get more tired than I do." This is true, and my argument holds no water.

"You and Bobby should be together. I get in the way." I say nothing, feeling more and more guilty.

The next day we leave in a rented car. "Ridiculous expense," she mutters. "I could have driven you myself so easily."

The last time I went to Franeker was in 1937, when, at the age of twelve, I accompanied my parents on an expedition to the small town where there was something miraculous: a modest-sized room in which the whole solar system — the earth, moon, sun, and planets — had been trapped by one man. Being totally unscientific, I never tried to fathom the workings of the wheels, cogs, and pendulums that made it work, but the thought that for hundreds of years the earth had been traveling around the sun in this little room, no matter what went on in the rest of the world, was marvelously reassuring and constant. As the years went racing by, I had kept that ordered microcosm secret in my mind, sometimes wondering whether I had imagined it, afraid to find that some disaster had shattered it. I had questioned people about it. What was the name of that shepherd of planets in Friesland? People drew a blank, mentioned tulips, dikes, Rembrandt, and had I heard about those dirty hippies in Amsterdam? To my mother, Franeker was the end of the world, a Nordic desert, and she recalled nothing of the captive constellations.

But during the summer of 1984 I found it. It is still there, ticking away as it has since the eighteenth century. The little golden balls dangle from the blue-green ceiling with its revolving planets; the gilt lettering indicates the signs of the zodiac, the leap years considered; the date, the hour are all measured as precisely as by the latest computer. And in this same room, in the closet bed, Mr. Eise Eisinga, who fashioned the planetarium, slept with his wife and children. A simple wool carder, he had taken seven years to build the wonder in his spare time. He had done it to educate a fanatic minister who was preaching doomsday in Friesland. The planets, predicted the preacher, were to collide on a certain date and cause the end of the world. Eise's construction showed that there was plenty of room in the heavens for the planets to bypass each other, and his fellow Frisians were reassured. Listening to the guide, I imagined

LEAP YEARS 217

the babies crying, the wife telling them not to touch Papa's foolish toy, and now she too has become one of my heroines, surely as devoted to genius as any artist's wife. It is said that she never objected to anything until he planned to lower one of the weights of his mechanism right through the family bed.

I describe it all to Mother in glowing terms when we return to Limburg. "You see, you don't actually have to travel all over the world," I tell her. "Eise Eisinga built his own space program right in his own room."

So now, edified, she does her best, undertaking intensive tourism in her backyard, seated first on the upper lawn, then beside the rosebush, and finally under the neighbor's tree. "I'm traveling, you see," she explains to passersby. "It looks quite different from here." And yet, when I casually mention our date of departure, she disappears for a whole morning and returns from town with a new traveling outfit. "You can drop me off somewhere on the way. In Paris perhaps I'll visit Jeanne. I'll be no trouble." To demonstrate her unwavering energy and fitness, she leads us on much too long a walk along the river, but the next morning she is frantically calling doctors. They prescribe another stay in the hospital.

She gives in, crestfallen and brave. Feeling like heartless monsters, we leave. Piloting us as fast as possible to Marseilles where we have a rendezvous, I insist nevertheless that we stop in the town of Beaune.

"What's in Beaune?" asks Bobby. I know that I was there in August 1938 and remember a vast room filled with beds. There had been little old men in the beds, and nuns like angels, wearing large starched coifs. "Some sort of hospital," I say now. "A kind of orphanage for old men." Confused by my own vagueness, I am nevertheless determined that we shall see it.

I have forgotten the extravagant Gothic architecture of the building, the ornate courtyard, the lacy spires and weather vanes. But the room is there, high-domed and airy as a church, the walls lined with wooden alcoves. Behind white curtains are the beds with red blankets and the bedside tables, on each one a polished brass spittoon—all intact, we are told, since the hospital's founding in 1452. The ceiling beams are painted and carved with grotesque animal heads, the floors paved with patterned tiles. Behind a latticework partition, opened every morning at Mass time, is a chapel. *Seulle* is written mysteriously all over the walls. *Seulle,* alone. Alone as my mother is in her efficient modern Dutch hospital, alone as is the great wooden statue of Christ wearing a heavy crown of thorns, His hands bound with rope, a death's-head under His foot. The dazzling triptych of the Last Judgment by Roger van der Weyden used to hang behind the altar. It is now exhibited in a separate room.

All this was planned and donated by a nouveau riche Burgundian named Nicolas Rolin in the fifteenth century. "Discarding all human pleasures to save only my soul . . . to the accommodation and assistance of the poor and the sick." What civilized charity, to provide the sick and the dying with such great works of art to look at! Yet now the little old men are gone, as are the nuns with the white-winged coifs. Is it likely that I really saw them here in their beds, sitting on these chairs? They had not seemed unhappy, suffering creatures to me then; on the contrary, they had had a merry air, like well-cared-for children, with clean pajamas and trim silver beards.

"In 1938 the patients were still here, I saw them," I tell the guide. Suddenly I feel ancient in front of all these tourists, as if I were a ghost from the fifteenth century. But the guide is not surprised. Not until 1971 were the patients moved to a modern hospital and the Hotel Dieu, like all other marvels of civilization, made into a museum. Perhaps culture, civilization, history are nothing but storage spaces for past treasures, a kind of memory bank for what is finished and dead, a museum run by curators and caretakers.

Now we speed through France, past cathedrals and castles, walled cities, and Roman ruins. We are on our way to verify a third memory of mine, the first man I ever loved. Eise Eisinga, Nicolas Rolin — I was right about them and congratulate myself on having had good taste at such an early age. But in Marseilles we will confront the real live hero of my adolescence, and the living are less reliable than the dead. They continue to change and refuse to be idealized.

Jean Alvarez has done well for himself. The penniless refugee in New York during the war has built, all on his own, a shipping empire spanning several continents. The news of his increasing millions has reached me through the years, mentioned with some irony by intellectuals, starving painters, and musicians, all supported generously by Jean. They seem to think it is uncivilized to earn money. "He works too hard," they say disapprovingly. "He's had one heart attack already." I expect to find a burned-out businessman, a despotic megalomaniac.

"You may not like him at all," I warn my husband, a man not to be ordered about. "He'll be the captain of the ship, the *maître à bord*."

But whether in his garden in Marseilles, at the dinner table over which his ninety-year-old mother presides, on the Lear Jet that flies us to his yacht, or on the walks we take along the deserted Turkish coast, Jean is first of all an exquisitely thoughtful host. "We will come to a cove in which the houses are drowned, the church is a ruin, and on the hill there are carob trees with a sweet fruit, a long pod with seeds in it. Do you smell the asphodel?"

The first day on board he spends with a Turkish mechanic installing a radio. Pieces of wiring cover the floor of the cabin. With knitted brows, the two men coax squeals and spurts of Moslem chanting out of the instrument.

When it is finally assembled, Jean's first call is to his mother. Jean, the rootless world citizen who in thirty years has not seen the four seasons consecutively in one locality, feels the need to check in daily with his mother, whom he has installed in the house in Marseilles where she was born. "Hello, Maman dear. The sky is blue. We're eating fish." And at the other end of the mysterious airwaves the aged voice exclaims, "What a marvel!"

I sit at his right at the table on deck under a blue awning. Across the table from him is his latest companion, an exquisite young girl of twenty-five, and beside her a portly gentleman, a childhood friend of his from before the war. The young girl knows nothing about that war, which lies between us like the table on which we are served our daily fish. On the wall of the cabin hangs a photograph of Jean in New York enlisting with de Gaulle's army at the age of seventeen.

"All the others were killed," he says, "and I'm still alive." His pout is still the same. His eyes darken briefly, as if there were some injustice in this, but at once the holiday that he has created here for us wins out. "Thank God!" he smiles, the sensuous curve of his lips still irresistible.

At times the excesses of his possessions seem to weigh on him. "I don't need two yachts," he mutters as his other vessel is sighted on the horizon. "Does any man need two?" But when it rises out of the sea with pennants flying, its wide, queenly bow breaking the waves with his youngest son at the helm and the two crews shouting at each other as the boats pass, going in opposite directions, he is jubilant. "Have you ever seen a more beautiful caique anywhere?"

After helping the sailors hoist the sail, he takes the helm. As he stands there, his brown, muscular back looks the same as when we swam in the lake in Connecticut. It is a brisk sail and we lie on our backs, marveling at the power of the wind and the strength of the tall mast. "Dolphins!" he cries triumphantly, pointing them out to us.

The meals are simple: chickpea soup, tomato salad with cheese, Turkish bread, and melons, and each time our host is appreciative of the tastiness of the food, congratulating the sailor who brings it up from the galley. Jean has not become jaded.

Toward evening he goes off with the three sailors to dive for fish, and returns with exotic specimens tucked in his bathing trunks. In the morning he gathers sea urchins, which he opens and serves up to us with a glass of raki.

He talks about his ranches in Argentina. "There was a gaucho who came to us, an old man. He slept outside under his coat. After a while I suggested we build him a lean-to, but he refused. '*Padre,*' I said, 'I want to build you a place to sleep because I love you.' The next day he disappeared and never returned." He looks at us with a kind of sorrow, and I can see the difficulty of being rich and generous. How hard it must be not to be resented for it.

"Once," he says, "I decided it was time to write my will, but immediately I burst into tears, so I never did."

His portly friend, who never passes an opportunity to poke gentle fun at him, exclaims, But what about his empire, the fleets, the houses, the art collection, the wives, the children? He shrugs. "There are laws. It will be fair. It's all theirs."

His art collection bothers him. "Why should I own all those things?" he says. His Courbets, Bonnards, and Monets are priceless. "One could run several hospitals with what they're worth." And yet the thought of a certain *Aphrodite* in the second room to the left in the museum in Athens moves him to tears. His description of the sky in a certain Canaletto is more eloquent than any artist's would be. In the same spontaneous way, he will suddenly recite entire passages of poetry we learned in school—de Vigny, Victor Hugo, de Musset—not with the pedantic cadences of a literary expert, but with the excitement of discovery. All these years have not dulled him. He has remained young.

Culture, to him, is not a question of sophistication but a kind of love affair.

Out there on deck, under the relentlessly blue sky, the days pass, serene and endless. Jean may sing the *Kreutzer* Sonata from beginning to end, or play gin rummy with the three sailors. Watching his friend float like a seal on his back, his rotund stomach rising like an island out of the sea, he shakes his head tenderly. "Poor Jacques," he murmurs. "He has just lost his father. It is hard on him."

With my husband he discusses navigation, endlessly and in technical terms, generous in acknowledging Bobby's expertise. Daily he ferries us ashore to the archaeological sites of incredibly old civilizations, talking about Mausolus and his wife, who built the first mausoleum, as if they were personal friends of his. As for himself, he wants no mausoleum. "When I die," he says, "I will not be remembered. You, Claire, you write books. You'll be immortal, but I, what did I do?"

He prides himself on not keeping any documents, correspondence, or mementoes. His desks and drawers are empty, he says. He will leave no revelations behind. Instead, he keeps looking ahead. "Goodness, there are still so many seas to sail: the Caribbean, the coast of Maine, the Baltic. Does anyone know the Baltic? What kind of fish could I catch there?" He talks about the houses he will buy, the children he may still have. As for the children he has had, grown sons and daughters, his previous wives, his grandchildren, he hardly mentions them. They are accomplished facts. Only his daily connection with his mother remains constant, via the wireless waves, an electronic umbilical cord. "Hello, hello. How are you, Mother dear?" And as her voice grows frailer I think of my own mother, unreachable now. I feel afloat, anchorless, but this sensation is liberating and not unpleasant.

Jean's young companion, on the other hand, diaphanous and elegant, talks only of the past: distant ancestors, their connection to various dethroned kings going back to the thirteenth century, the family archives, eccentric great-uncles living in crumbling castles. She survives on nothing but fish heads and watermelon and her eyes have an eerie opalescence, like moons. Her youth worries him, he confides in me. "Just think," he says, his eyes darkening. "When I'm seventy and getting decrepit, she will be only thirty-seven. Is it fair to her?" And yet of the two he seems to be the source of energy. His vitality overwhelms us all.

"Come, come on deck." He rouses us up in the middle of the night. "The stars are falling. You can make wishes. It's a unique opportunity."

There, in a dark cove sheltered by incredibly high cliffs, we lie side by side on the wide afterdeck and he offers us stars as if they were invaluable tips on the stock exchange. "Excuse me for waking you up," he says, apologizing. "But could you bear to miss it?"

I think of that summer night exactly forty years ago when I stood at the bedroom window of the cottage in Connecticut and he waved at me across the web of moonlight. I had been right to love him. My friendship with him now is easier. I am no longer afraid of losing my identity, of being absorbed by his overwhelming one. The difficult strain of being in love is no longer gnawing at me like a toothache. He shares with us this yacht, this sea far removed from anything I have ever known, this coast, these ruins of distant, ghostly cultures. Lying there on deck, we're in love with the world, its fishes, its stars, its crickets, the spicy smell of asphodel, with time itself, which is both meaningless and yet perfecting all things, the crucible in which our lives have been distilled.

Tomorrow our vessel will lift anchor and move on, leaving no trace here. The light falling from the sky is bright and Jean's young girlfriend, who has been reading Proust all day, curled up in windy corners of the boat, drowning in her masses of Venetian red hair, reads us a description of the Duc de Guermantes at eighty-three years old: "as if men were perched on top of live stilts, growing continuously, sometimes taller than church towers, from which height, suddenly, they fall." Then her voice trails off as if nothing more need be said.

Tonight my stilts have grown long enough with years so that I can look beyond my familiar horizons. This Turkish coast is far removed from Holland or Long Island, Europe or America. This sky seems closer than the earth. On Jean's yacht, roots seem for the first time irrelevant. Piloted by him, I can imagine taking off into space for another world with no regrets. Then the image of my mother, as old as the Duc de Guermantes, suddenly appears to me on giant stilts, as tall as the masts of the craft. On them she is leaping over imaginary fences, taking off between the stars in search of the ones that just plummeted through the sky. No doubt she will find them and gather them in her baskets, a cosmic gardener, a confectioner of constellations. From her superior height she laughs down at me. "Did you think you could simply take off, forget all about me, leave me buried in my garden?" How cleverly she has spanned my trajectory from Eise Eisinga's claustrophobic microcosm, through Rolin's ideally civilized home for the dying, to this stellar escape of Jean's, still keeping me captive within her orbit.

23
SHELLS

"It will not be convenient for you to begin dying before the sixteenth of March," I tell her on the telephone.

"All right. Come on the seventeenth and then I'll start."

"Can you wait till the nineteenth? I'd like to stop over in London for a day. From there I'll take the boat, a slow boat. I will arrive at ten P.M." I am stalling for time. This is one trip I do not want to take.

"I won't be able to meet you at the train."

"That's all right. I'll take a taxi." I can manage on my own. She can no longer manage on her own. Finally, finally she needs me. She will allow me to help her die. She will show me how; she will teach me. She will do it well, exceptionally well, as she does all things. *"Il faut bien faire les choses,"* her mother used to say. The boat sails through a sea that is gray like the sky. It takes me away from the land of the living. Are we crossing the Styx into Hades? I am afraid of what I shall find, yet how impatiently she lies waiting. She decides to stop drinking liquids so that I will not have to wait too long. She must be glad now that I am taller than she, towering over her, so I can carry her in my arms like a small bundle. My mummy, all bone, all spikes like the frilled dogwinkle shells lying on the windowsill, all nose like a plucked bird, all eyes, all soul, or whatever it is that swims to the surface when she looks at me and cocks her small head sideways and tells me she is happy, that heaven is here, on earth, in this room.

Then the days pass. Endless they seem as we sit side by side on the sofa, wide-eyed and watchful. I call Sylvia who is now living in New Hampshire and tell her to come, even though Mother forbade her to some months ago. "I have no profound statements to make on my deathbed," she told her then. Now she longs for her and Sylvia undertakes the journey, which lasts, after all, no more than a night of fitful sleep, a day without meals, during which I bring Mother lemon peels, freesia blossoms, crushed mint leaves, all with scents she avidly inhales.

Jeanne arrives from Paris, looking so strong that I'm afraid she will crush her younger sister to her bosom. She wipes tears from her eyes. "She's a saint," Jeanne whispers to me and I smile at this, coming from that difficult aunt who has now stopped judging, dazzled by Mother's simplicity, her determination.

A priest comes. She has asked for him. "There must be something else, something besides this body," she says. "Tell him to wear his robes." But it is Jeanne who answers the prayers in perfect Flemish, the language of her childhood, which she has not spoken since. Nothing is forgotten. These rites, performed so long ago at the side of my great-grandfather's bed, are important, even if they have been ignored during a lifetime.

The Dutch priest, though dignified and kind in his white surplice, is too liberal, too brief. In ten minutes it is all over. The candles are blown out and he drives off in his car. I feel something is missing and sing a song that floats up out of my own childhood — "Lord Jesus has a garden where sweet flowers grow." And another, taught to my father by Bonne Maman:

> On three kings day in the evening
> A ship sailed into the harbor
> In which Mary Magdalen sat.
> And they played to her on the organ,
> And they sang to her the song.
> Your sins are forgiven no matter how great
> And Christ shall be believed.

Finally we are alone, Mother and Sylvia and I. It is raining. It is Palm Sunday. A fly buzzes in the room. "Don't hurt her. She's a well-behaved fly called Fifi, an old friend," Mother says.

She asks for tea with a lump of sugar and wets her lips in anticipation. Sylvia draws her portrait and she dozes off. In the little whitewashed room, the bed with the swans is like a ship on which the three of us will sail forever — out of time and space — on that gray sea, through that gray sky separating us from the land of the living. Yet on this voyage Mother sails alone. How disconcerting to be left behind with an empty shell that is not her, that is cold and foreign and white and still, wearing a silk scarf that once belonged to Bonne Maman, wrapped in a linen sheet from her grandmother's house, The Rose, in St. Truiden, objects preserved from generation to generation to knit us all into a history, the continuation of which is now left in our hands.

Within two weeks Sylvia and I have torn her life apart and will transport its mementoes once more to America. The house is stripped of furniture. Our children have claimed the Venetian glasses she and Father bought on their honeymoon and Bomma's blue and white soup tureen, in which she served the broth on Sundays. My

oldest son must have the ram's horn on which his grandfather used to blow to call him in for supper. I have claimed
the bed with the swans in which I was born, and Sylvia will
be using Mother's sculptor's tools and Father's ancient
books on heraldry and iconography to continue the atavistic craft of stained-glass painting in a technological world.
Nothing must be forgotten.

Father's paintings are taken down from the walls, the
drawers are emptied of postcards from holidays in Florence, the first in 1917, the last in 1983, and all the holidays
in between — to Mexico, Spain, France, California.

The neighbors come and pick through the boxes. "How
can you throw away a thermometer and a perfectly good
meat grinder?" Apologetic, I take them back. They carry
away art books and empty jam jars. Nobody claims the
leather pouch with the silver buckle, nor the brown sweater
we bought together in 1980.

When no one is looking, I throw away the negatives of
snapshots, piles and piles of them, and feel guilty: the
Sunday poet in a deck chair in the garden of the house by
the sea; Mother shielding her eyes from the sun, sitting
next to him, wearing a necklace of shells; my sister and I
wearing matching pointed hats, frowning at the camera;
Father as a very young man installed in front of a ploughed
field, painting; Mother again in the Piazza San Marco,
wearing a sleek coat with a fur collar, one button on the hip,
and a hat with a slanting brim. How beautiful she was, how
young. Suddenly the sadness of all this youth and beauty
vanished overwhelms me and angrily I tear up this negative
too. There is no time to look, to linger, no time for senti-
ment. My own life is running out and I must not pore over
the past another minute, must no longer allow material
things to tug at me.

Sylvia is more generous. She still loves objects. She still
longs to hold the small statue with the pointed buttocks
brought back from Africa by my father's older brother

Charles, to own Bomma's precious plates with the small ladybugs on them, one perfect tulip at their center. I want to sell. I'm hardening. My children need money. Of the art nouveau salt cellars from Brussels, the four Delft gin glasses with spirals climbing inside their stems I say, "Sell! Or take them. They're yours." I long to own nothing ever again, to be stripped of possessions.

Then the house is quite empty, hollow like the frilled dogwinkles that Mother painted less than a month ago — insignificant, dusty things transformed by her attention, her eyes and hands into an important statement, I know not of what: houses left behind by long-decayed mollusks? Something that remains and still echoes of the sea?

These empty rooms are no longer hers; she is already far away. One could start all over here with nothing but a mattress and a saucepan to one's name. One could build up a whole new life, accumulate different possessions, new snapshots. I sweep away the dust. The walls are white and bare. It is almost gay. I long to dance in this space.

How efficient we have been, how clever. We didn't even fight, Sylvia and I, as we used to over the respective talents of our young men. On the contrary, we have become as close again as when we were children and she would take me by the hand to cross dark corridors, braver than I though three years younger. At night, she was the one who told me stories to lull me to sleep, endless stories, to be continued.

Now we work like mature, decided women, side by side, so we can return as soon as possible to our real lives over there, to our husbands and children and our children's children. Yet sometimes they seem very distant, very unreal, for they do not call us, do not seem to need us, while we struggle to shed this past of ours in order to be free, to be solidly transplanted at last, unhampered by nostalgia and memory. Perhaps they do not need us and we might as well stay here in this riverbed and walk together through the long late Nordic evening, through the green meadows, and watch the boats labor by, dragging their heavy bellies past the shores of the Maas.

How contagious the sound of all these bells, still ringing their madly Catholic clamor from convents and monasteries now only thinly populated. Perhaps their message is still valid. It might be sweet to age here together, sharing this world we loved once. The people greet us as if we had never left, finding us vaguely familiar, somewhat younger echoes of our mother. In the cozy cafés we are welcomed at the tables covered with Persian rugs. Young men buy us beer. When we leave everyone kisses. Three times is the custom, a feast of kisses, a sweet, all-embracing communality we shall not find again.

She left all this without regret. "They say one meets all those one has ever loved over there," I ventured timidly, offering comfort, but she, matter-of-fact, with a wicked twinkle answered "Heaven forbid!" and lying on her side dove into a bottomless sleep.

And yet she used to say, "I live in a hollow, but I love my hollow," about this spot of land, which is periodically flooded by the high waters of the Maas. Now the shell is empty but the garden has burst once more into bloom. The moss-covered statue of the woman still leans over, dipping her hair into the green. On the roof of the house facing the west, to which we shall fly away presently, is perched that other creation of hers, the silhouette of a mermaid blowing on a conch and swimming off into the sky. I know that no matter where I am, no matter how high the waters rise, I shall hear its call.